THIS BOOK BELONGS TO

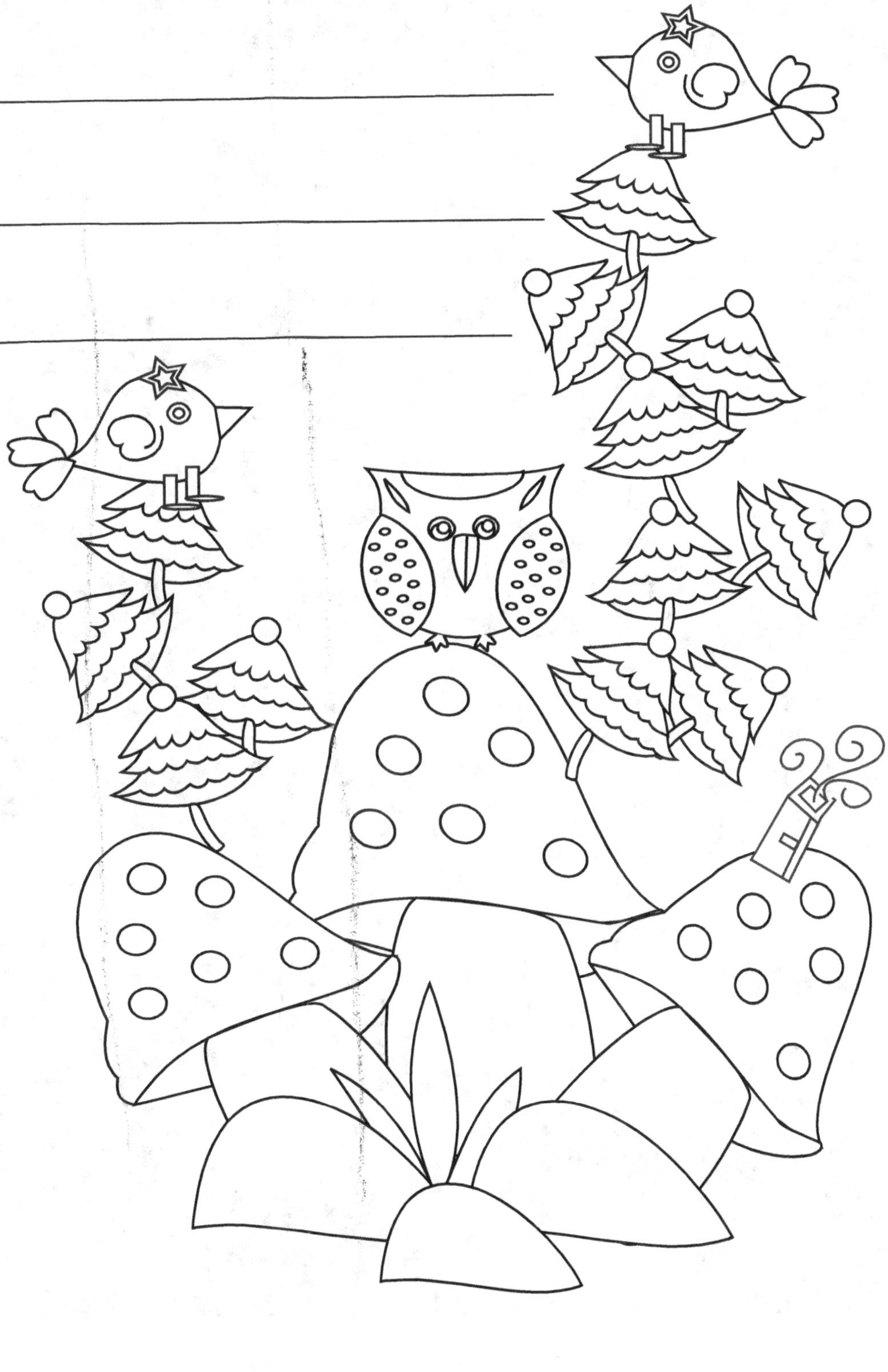

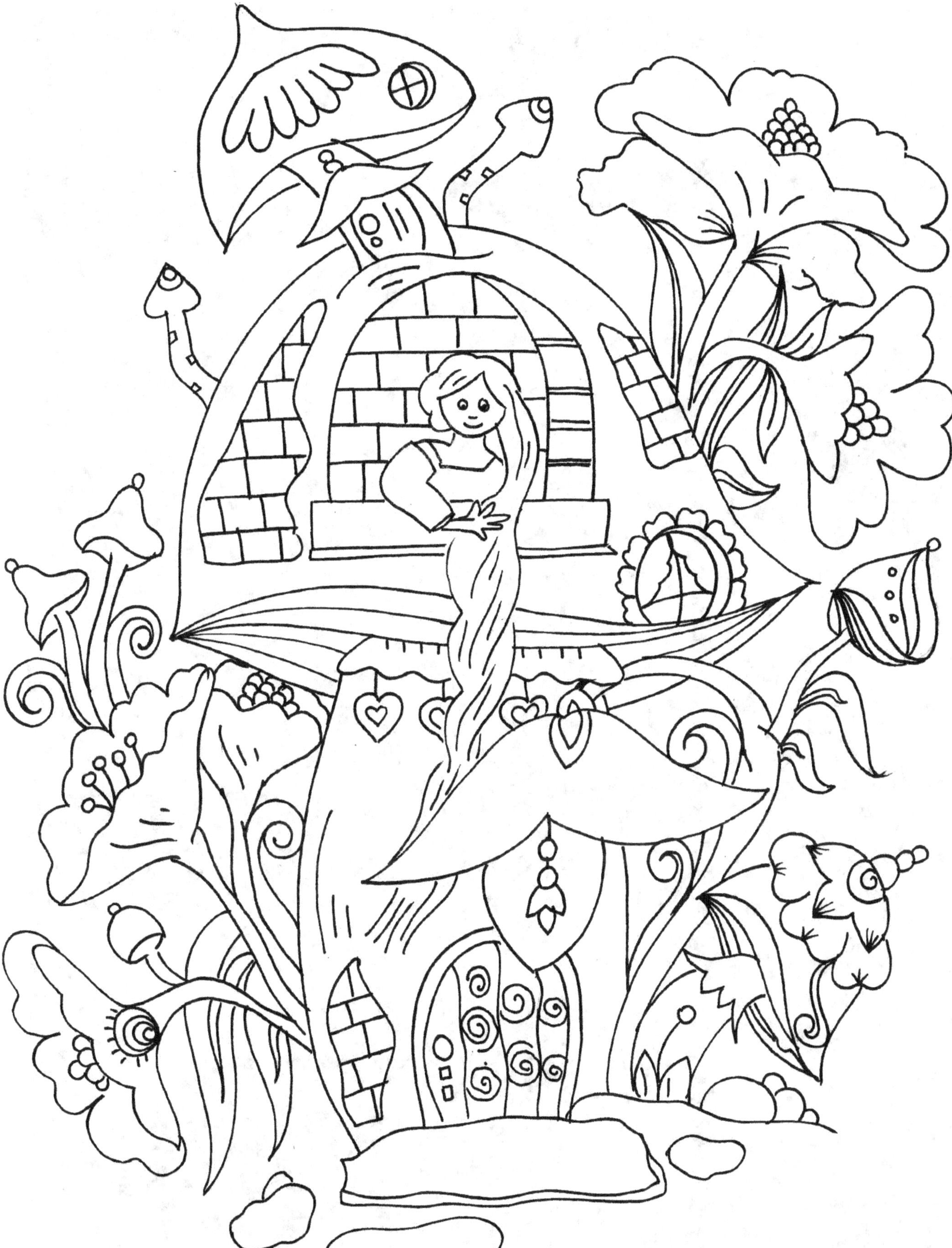

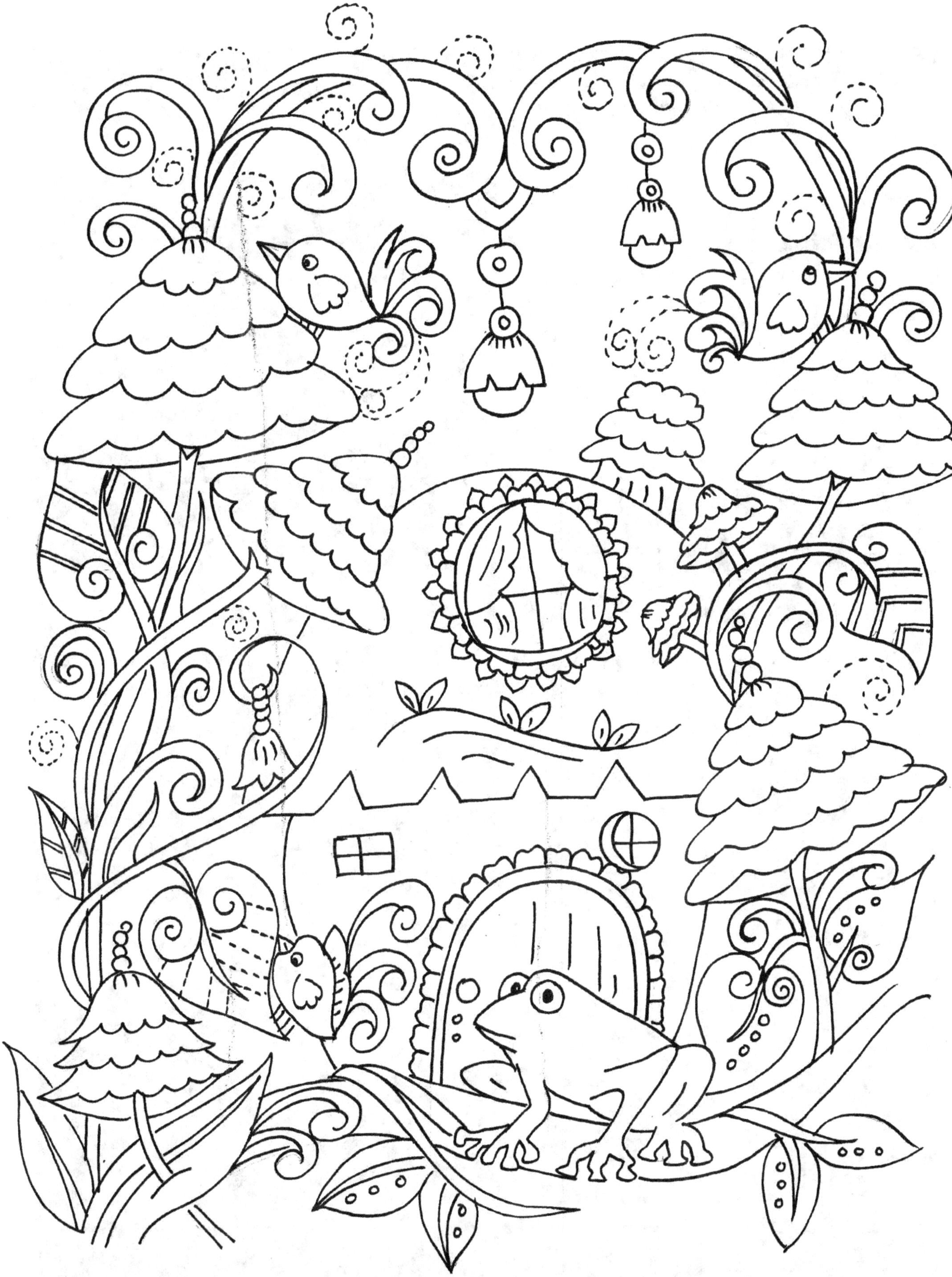

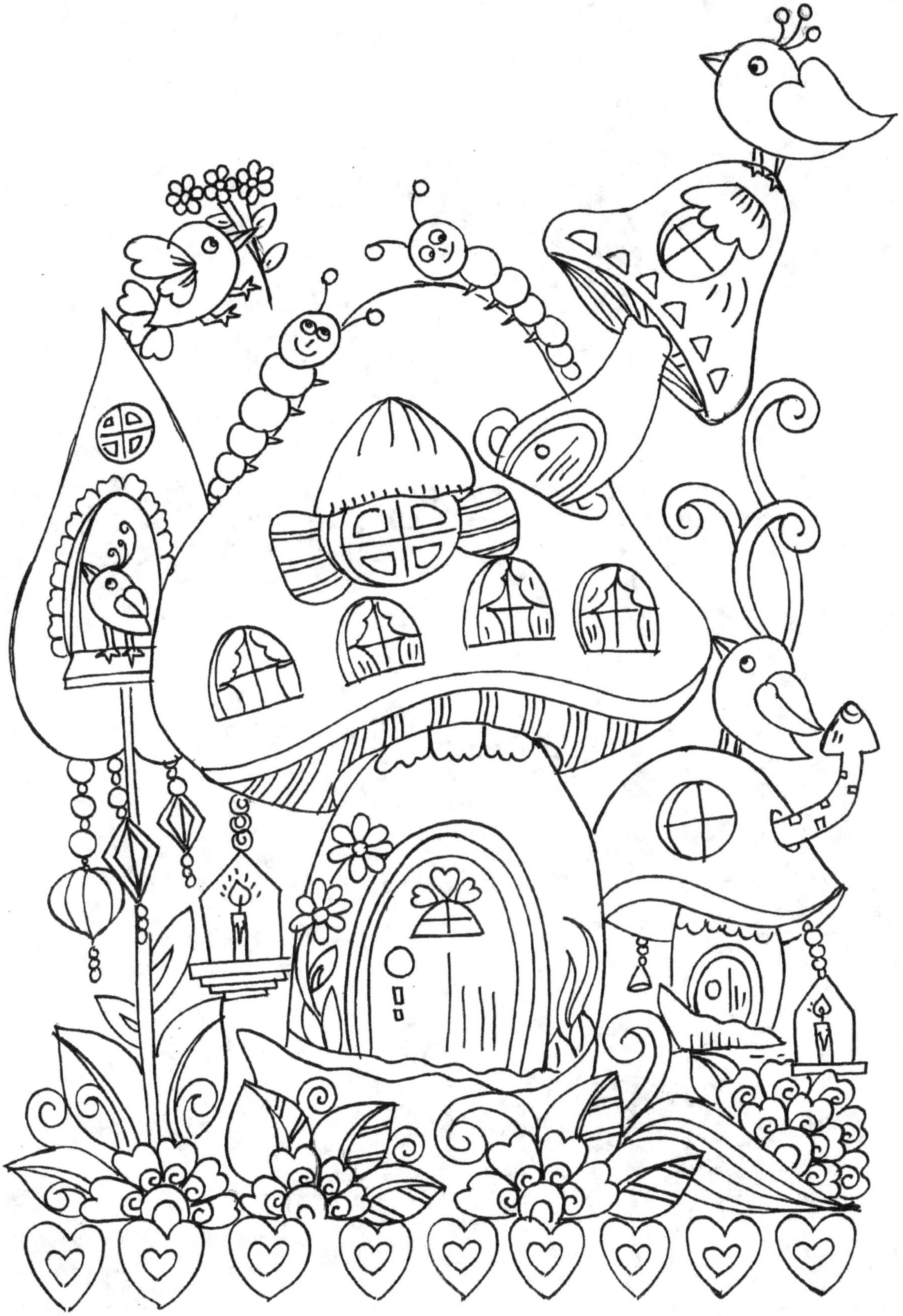

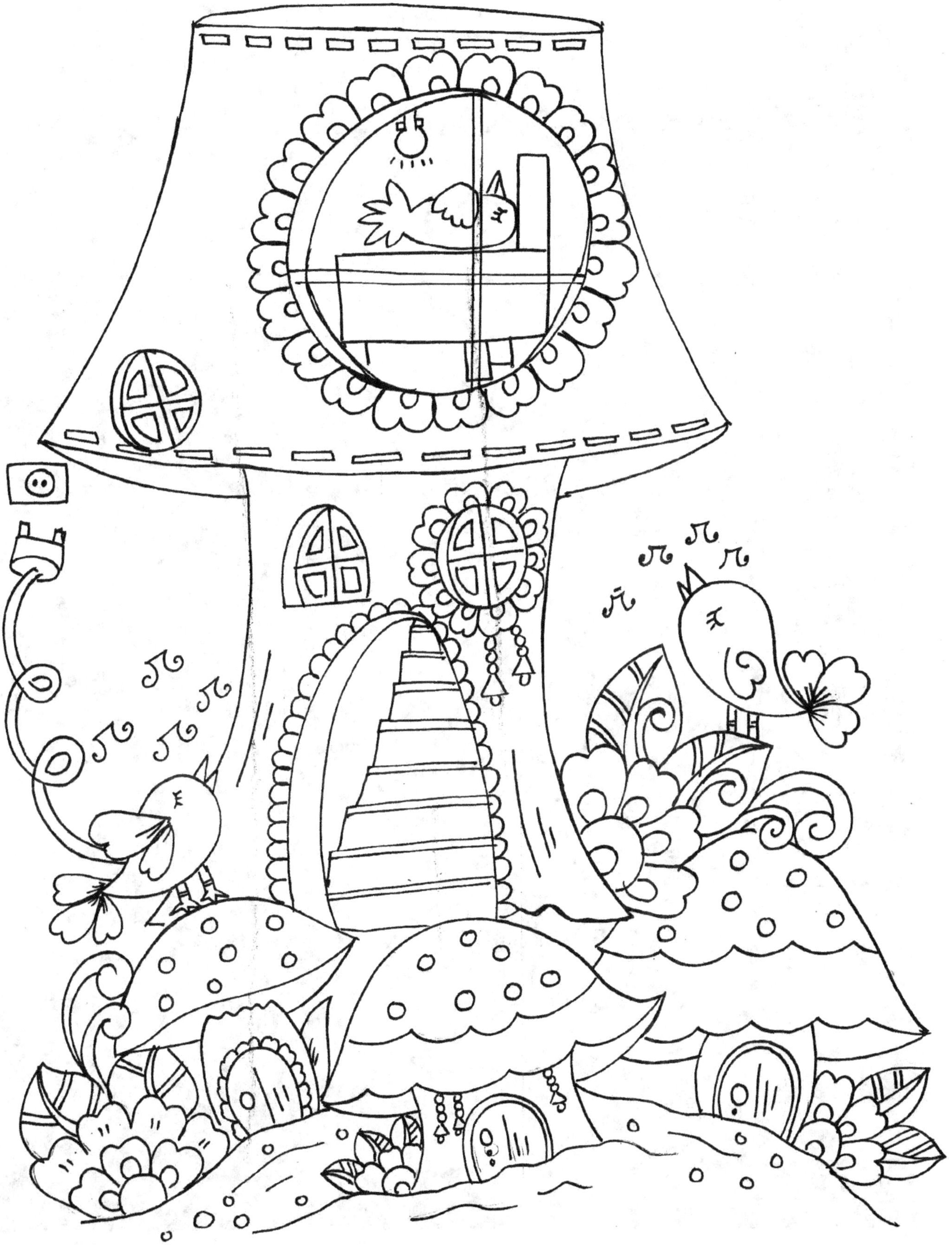

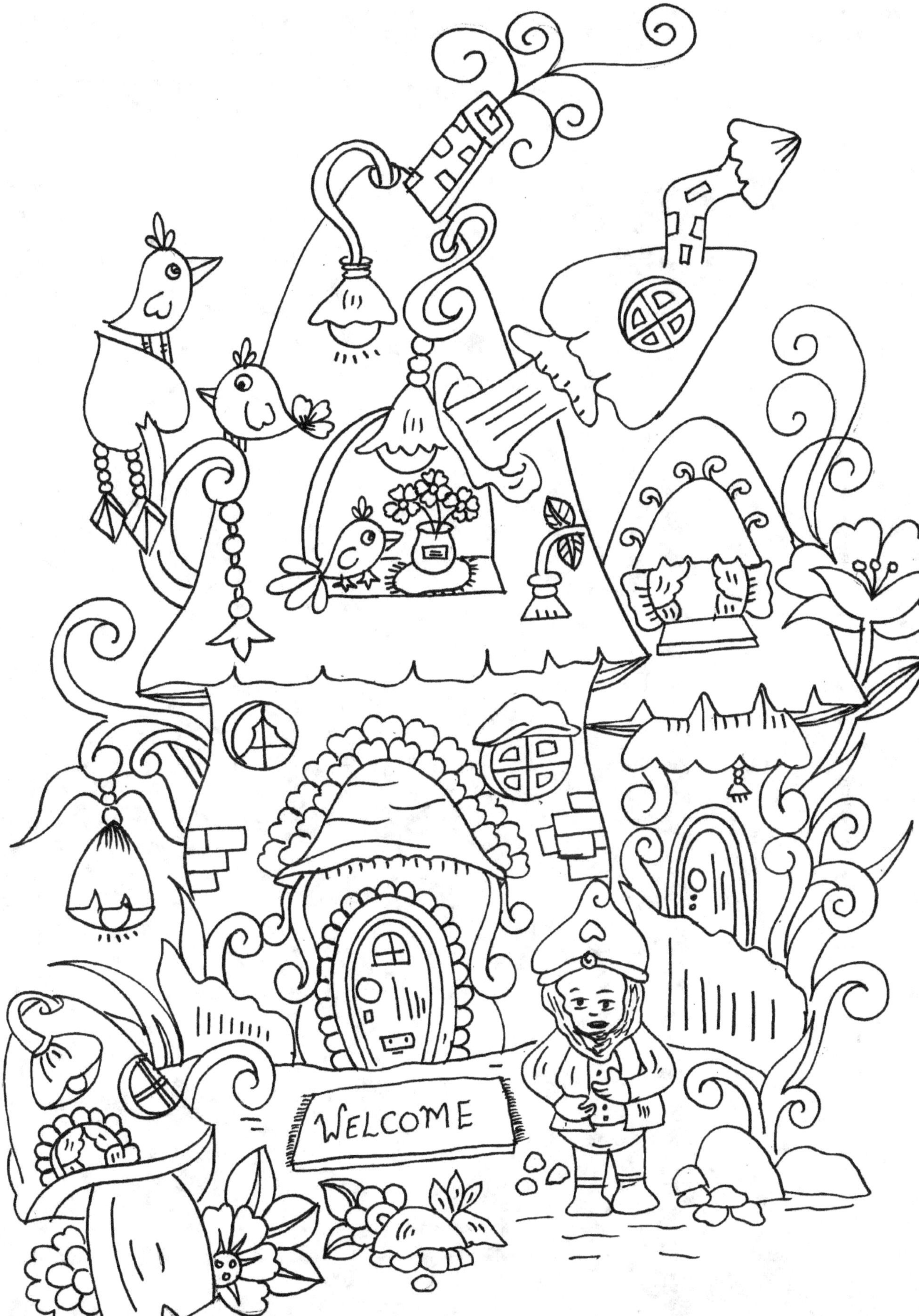
WELCOME

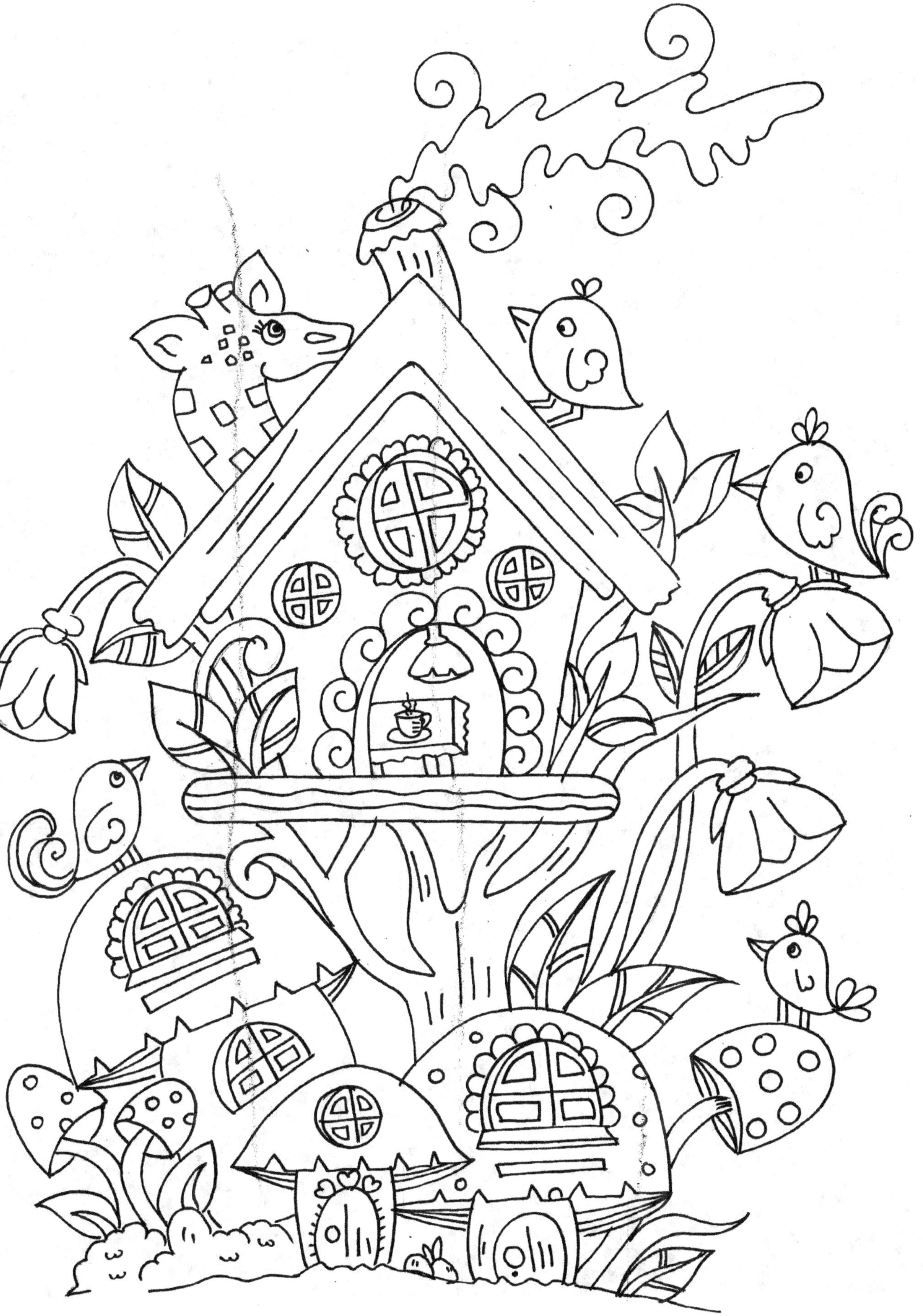

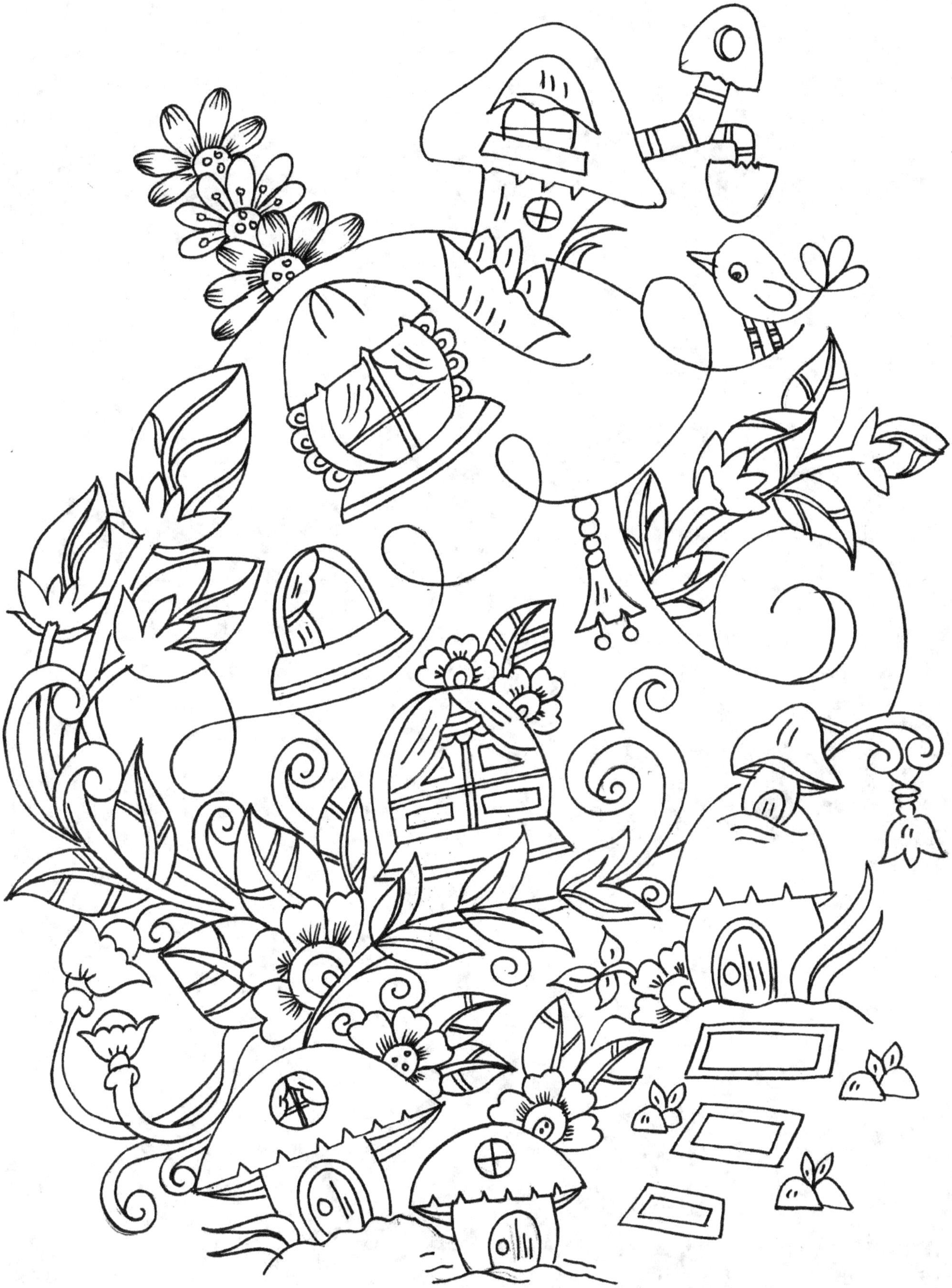

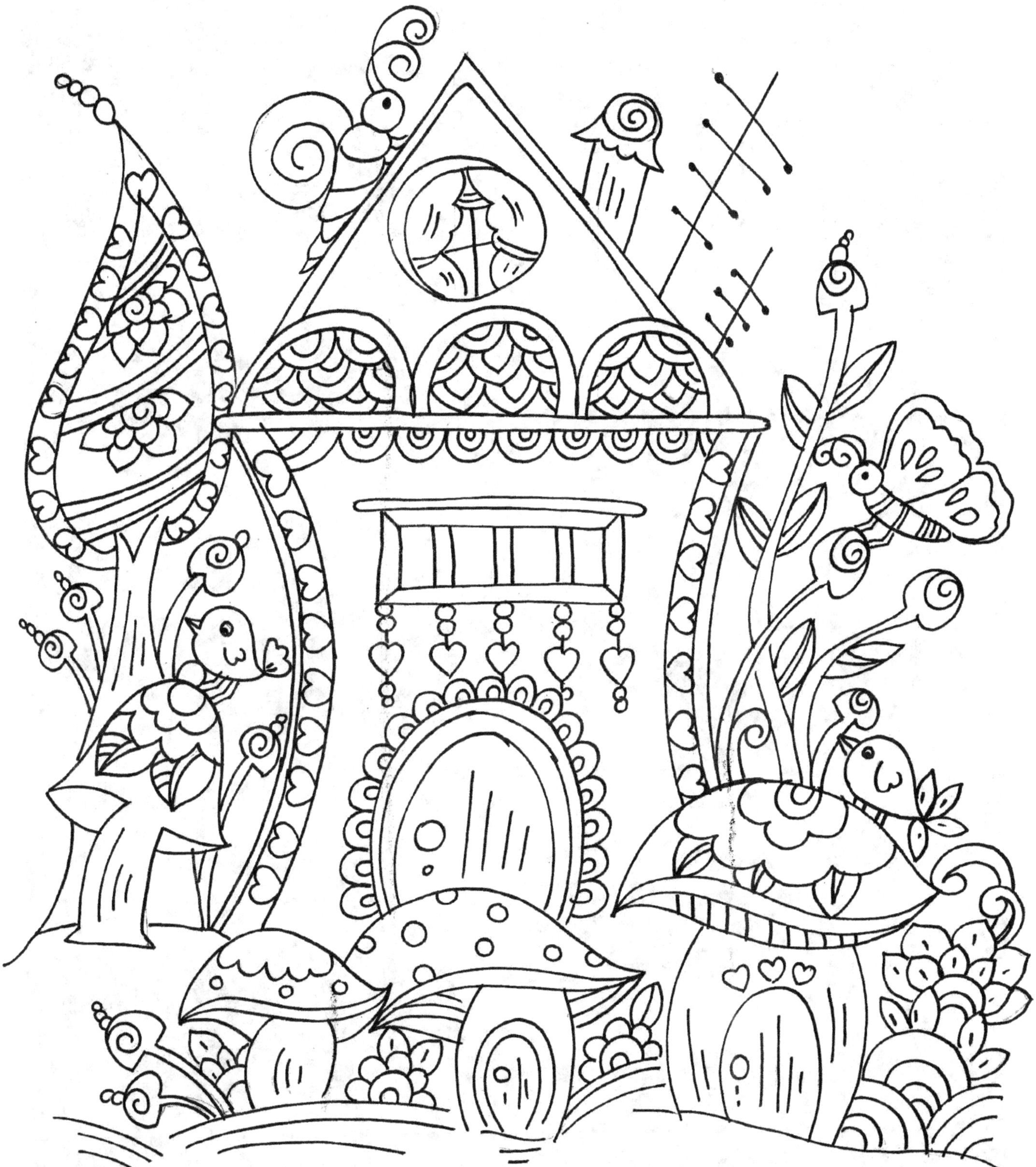

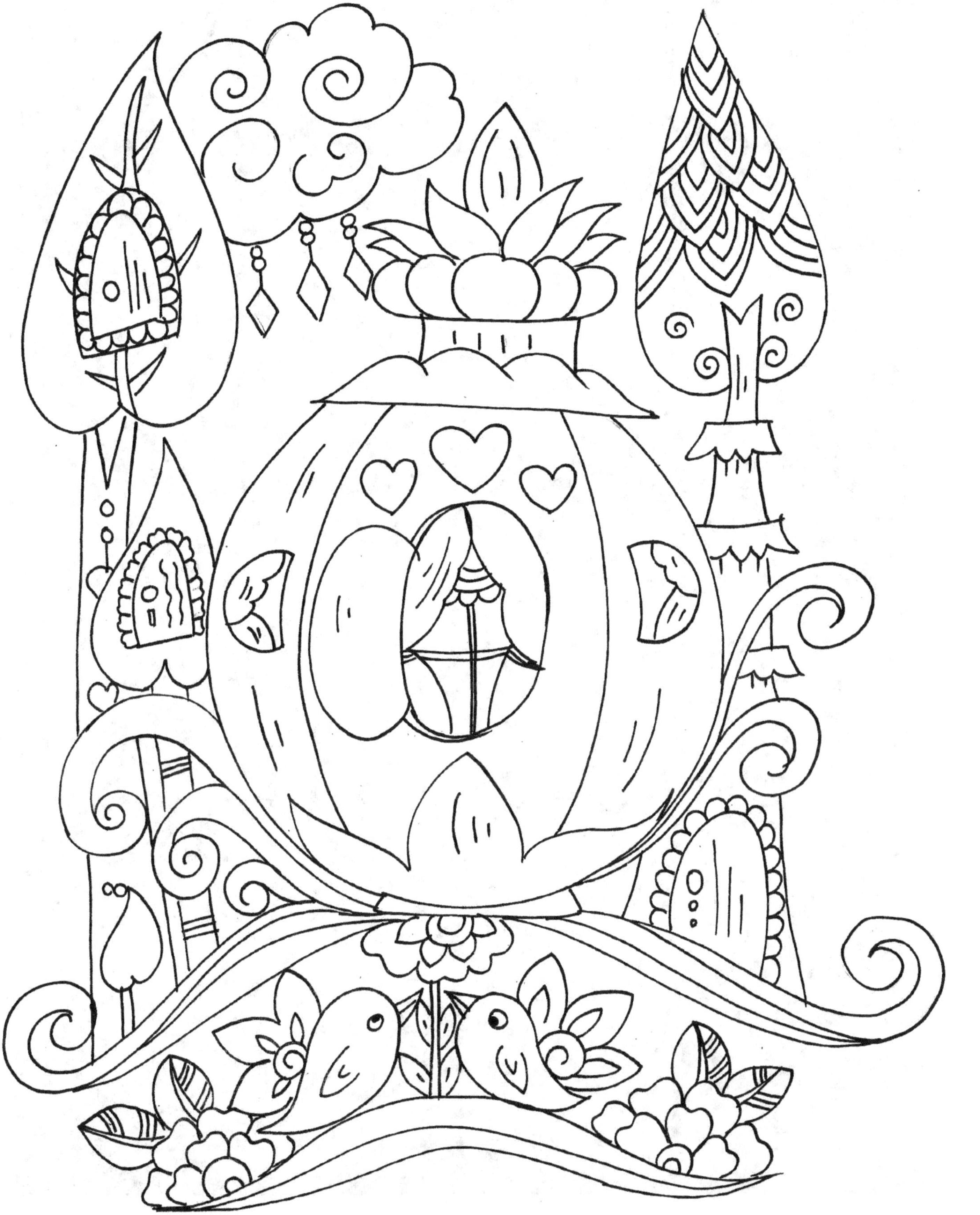

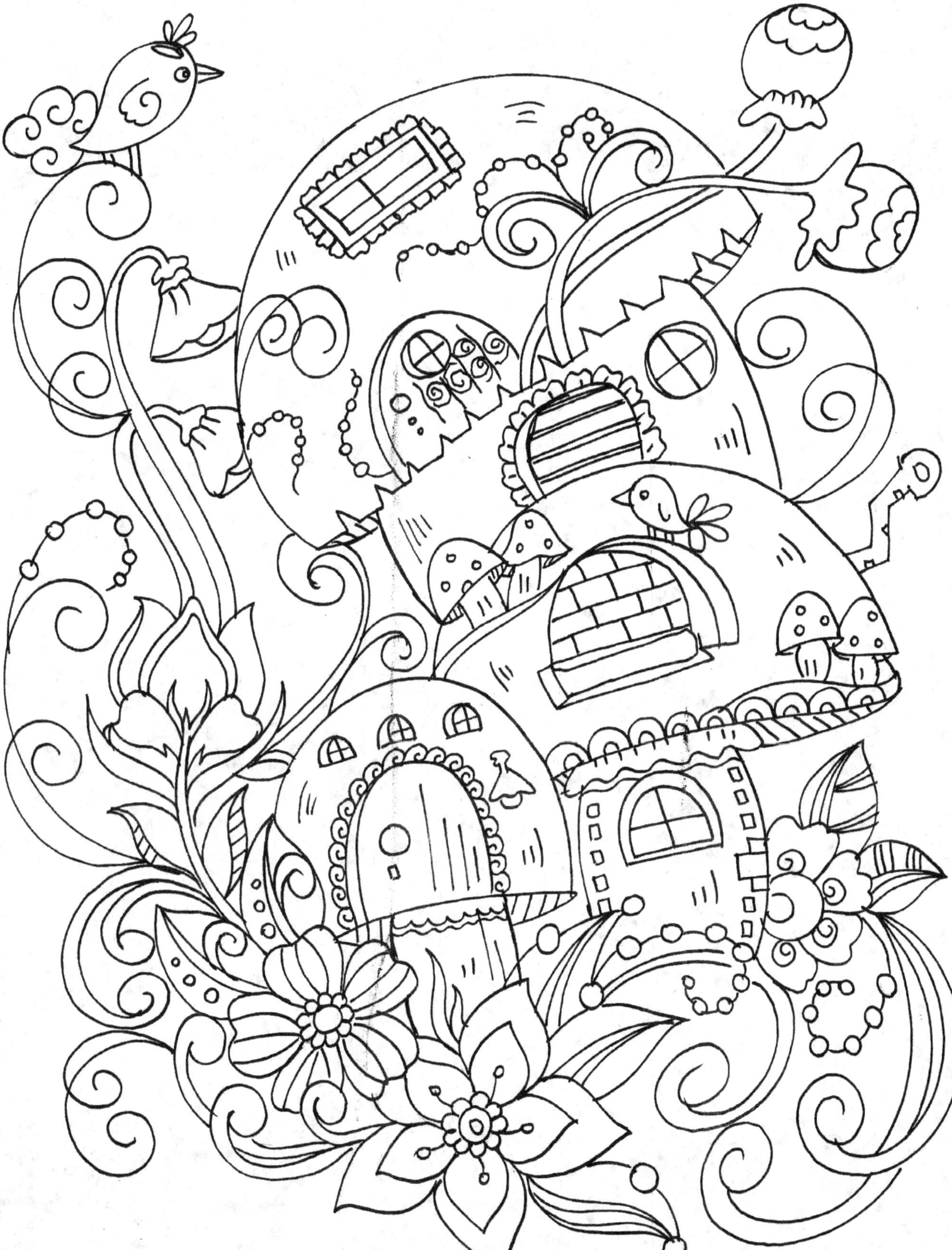

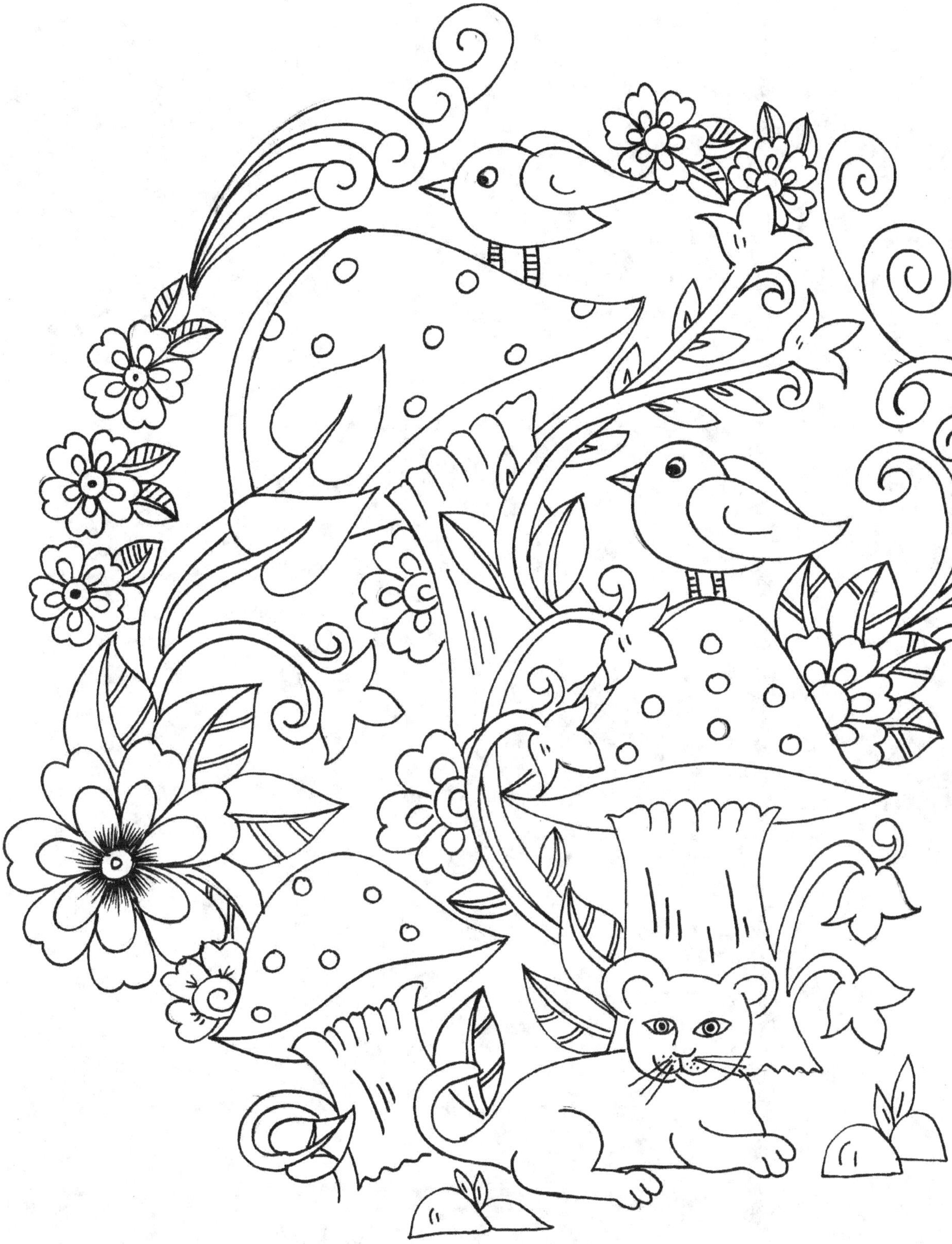

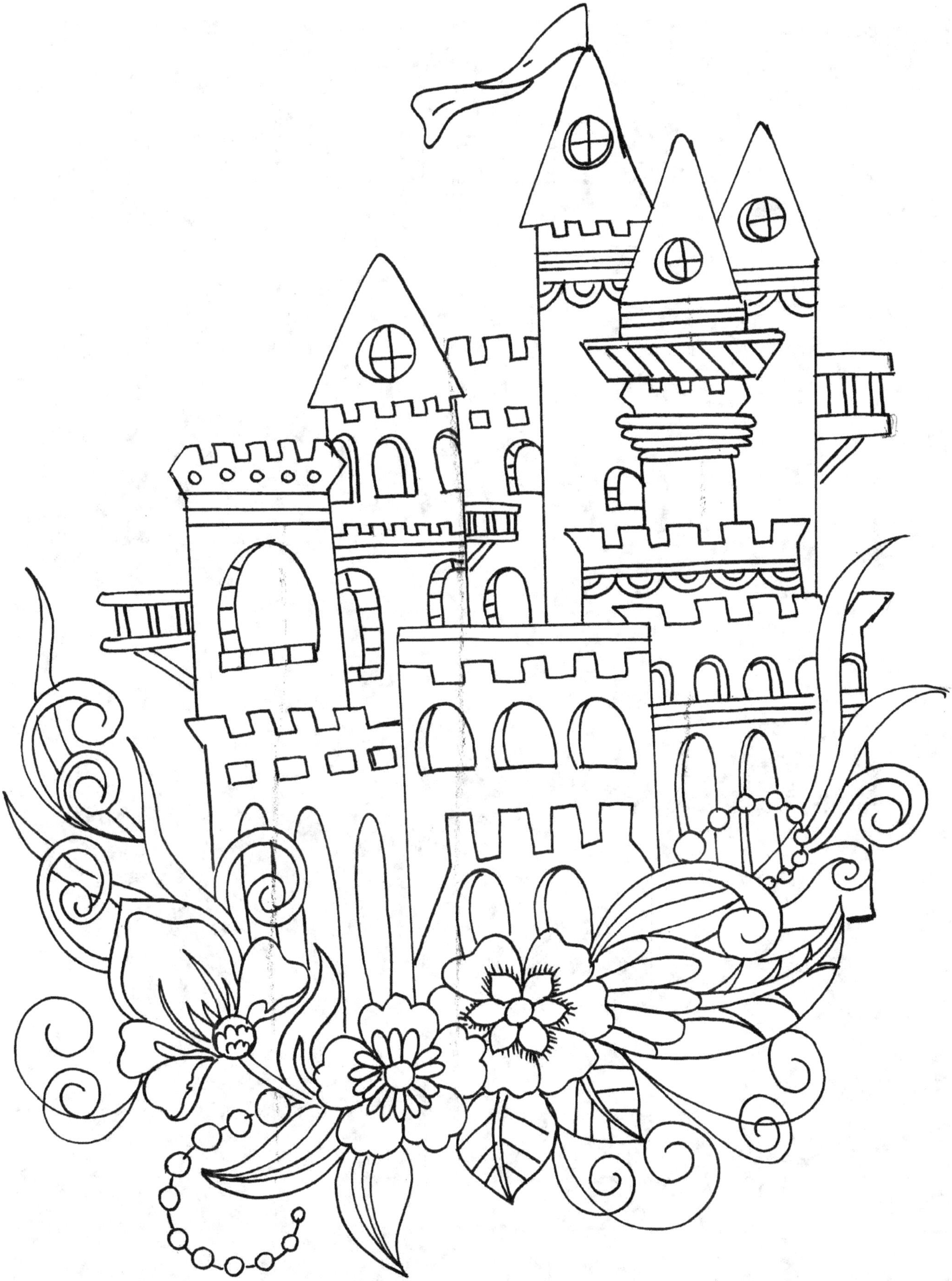

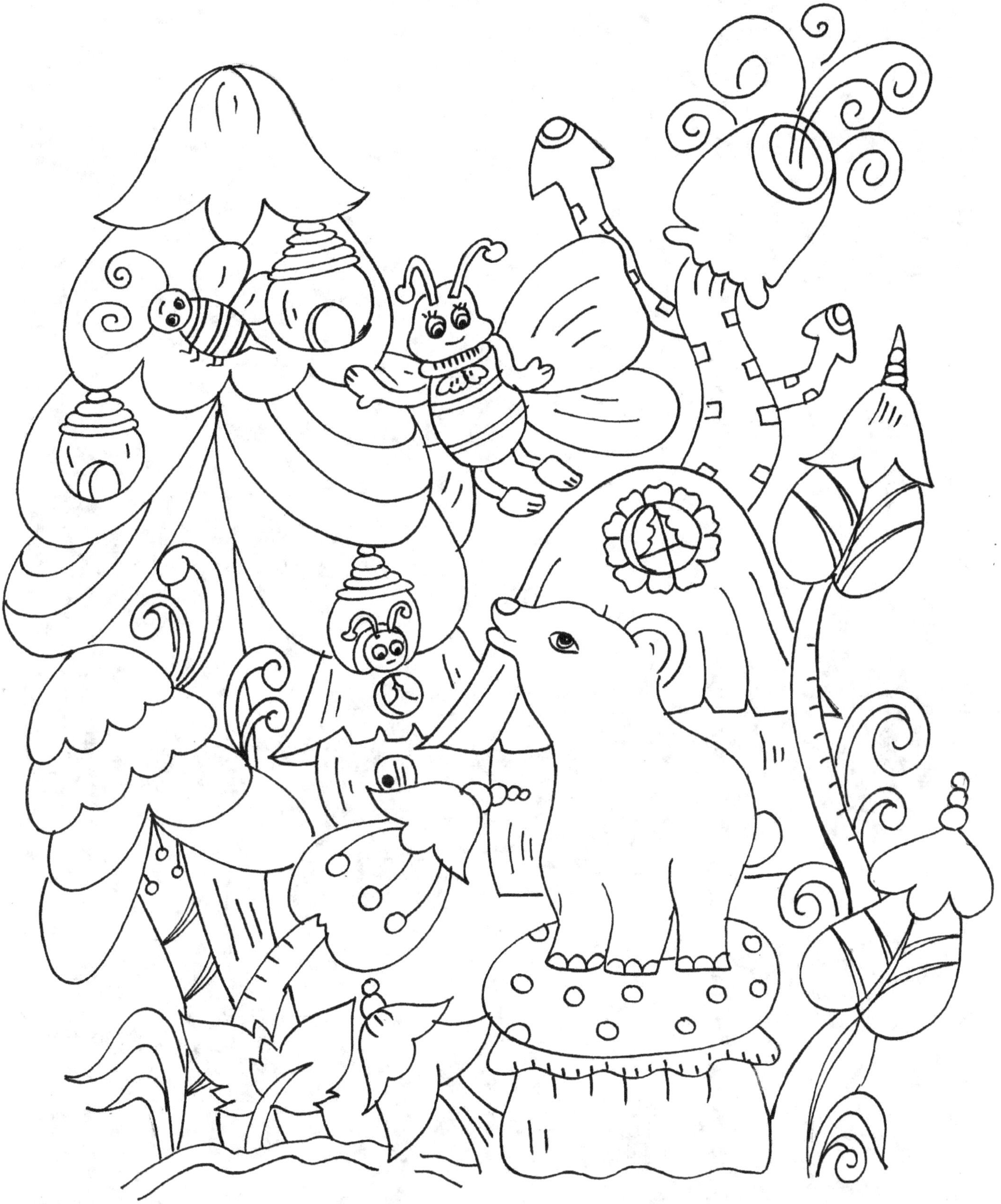

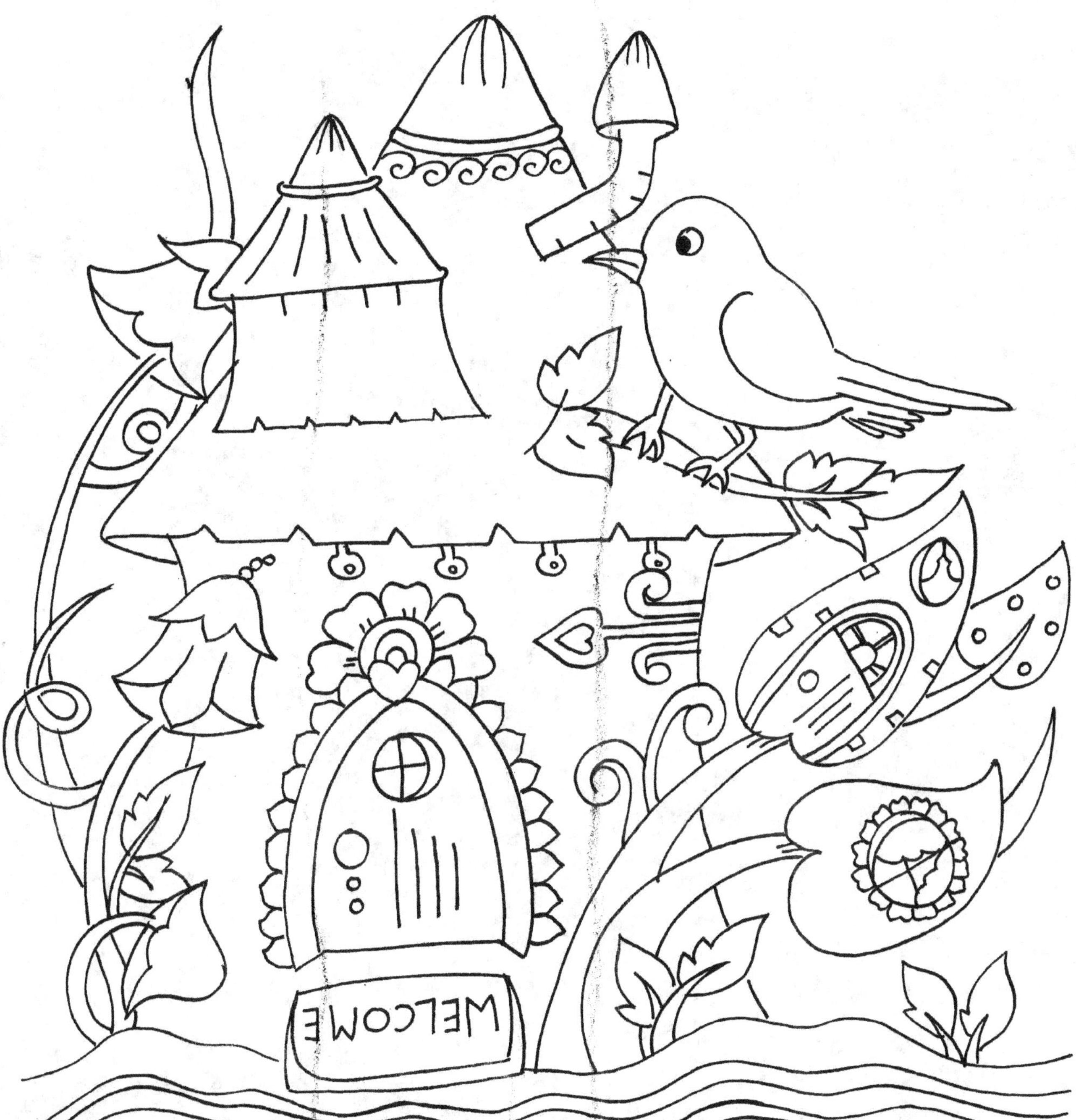
WELCOME

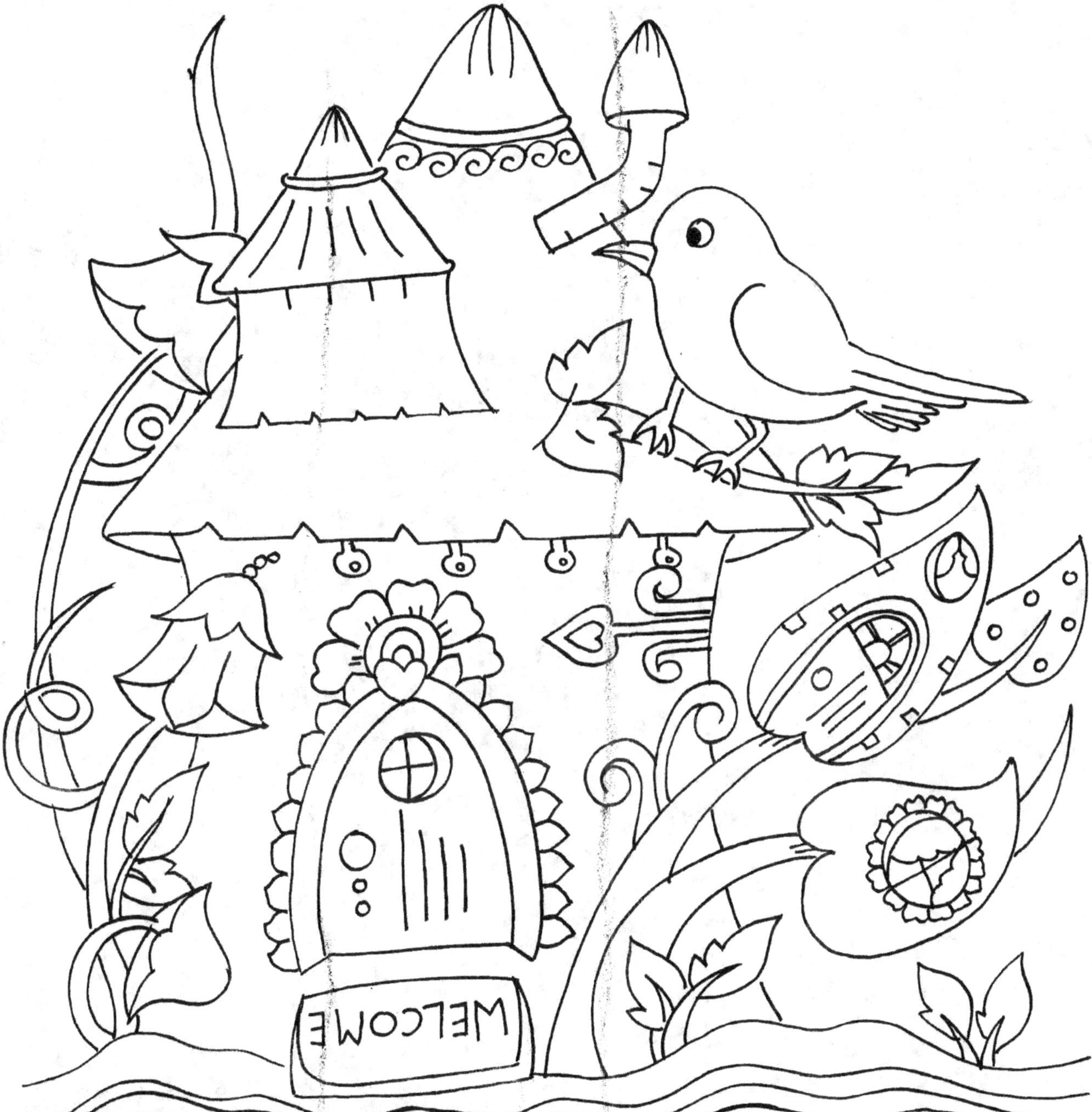
WELCOME

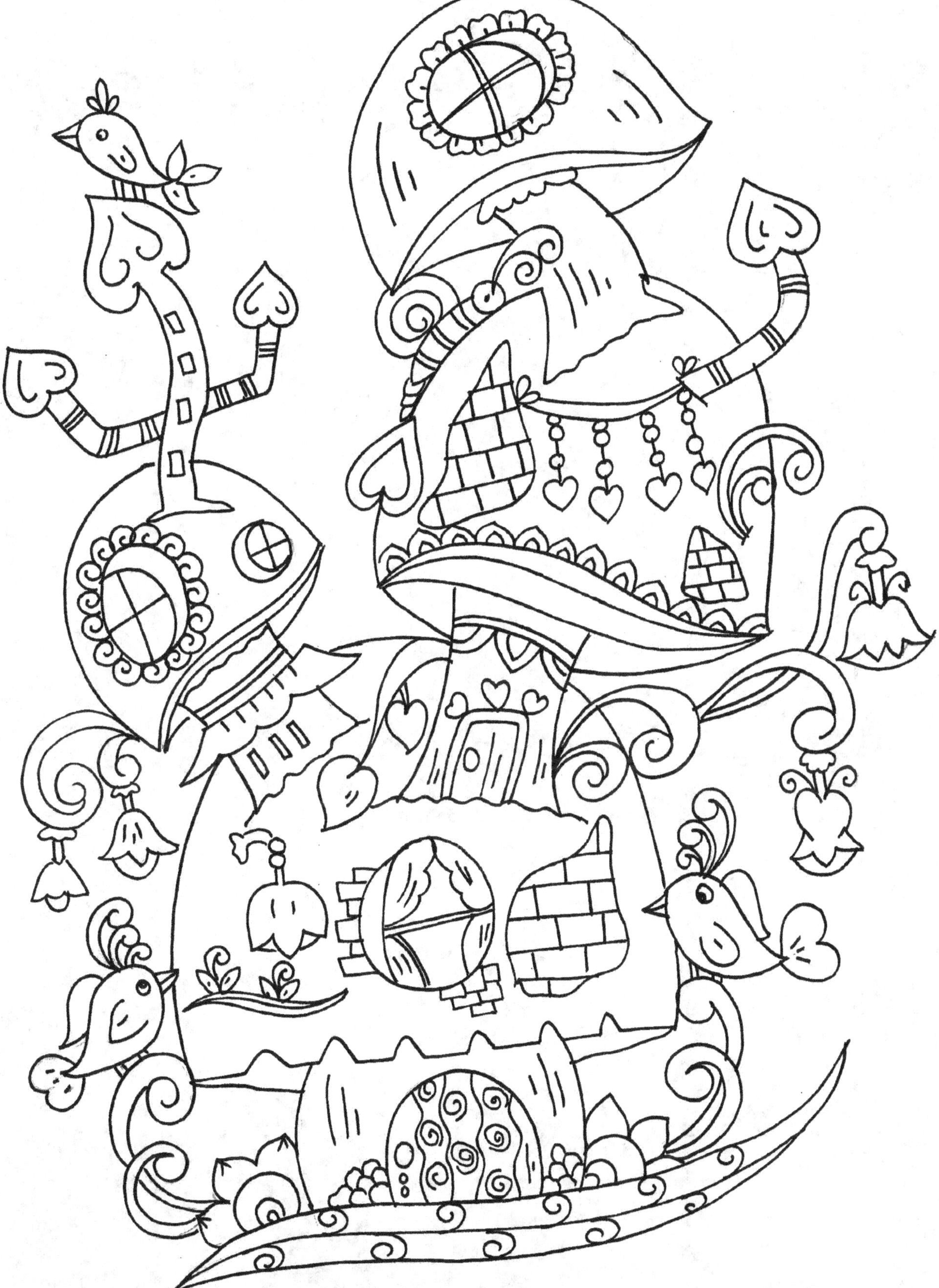

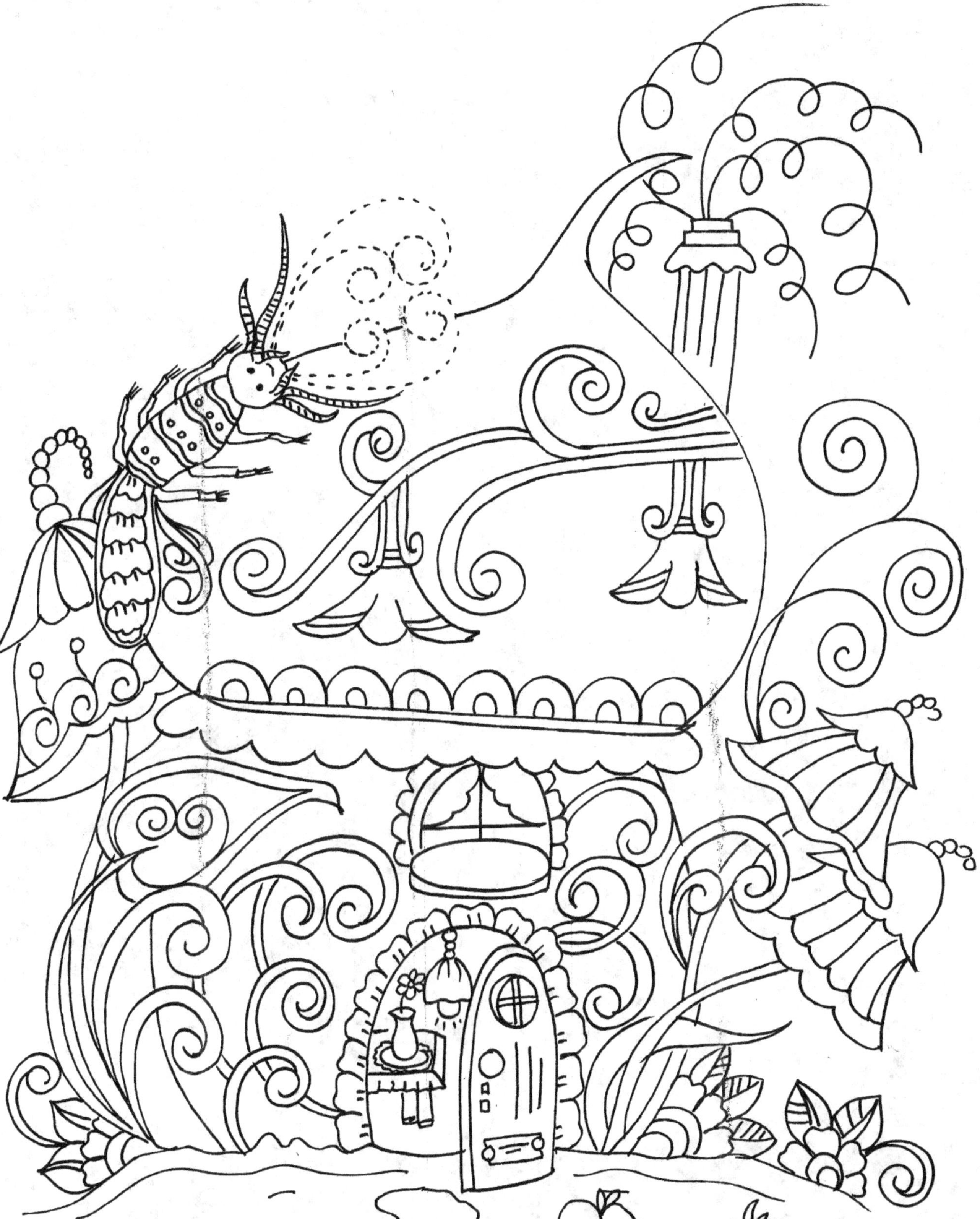

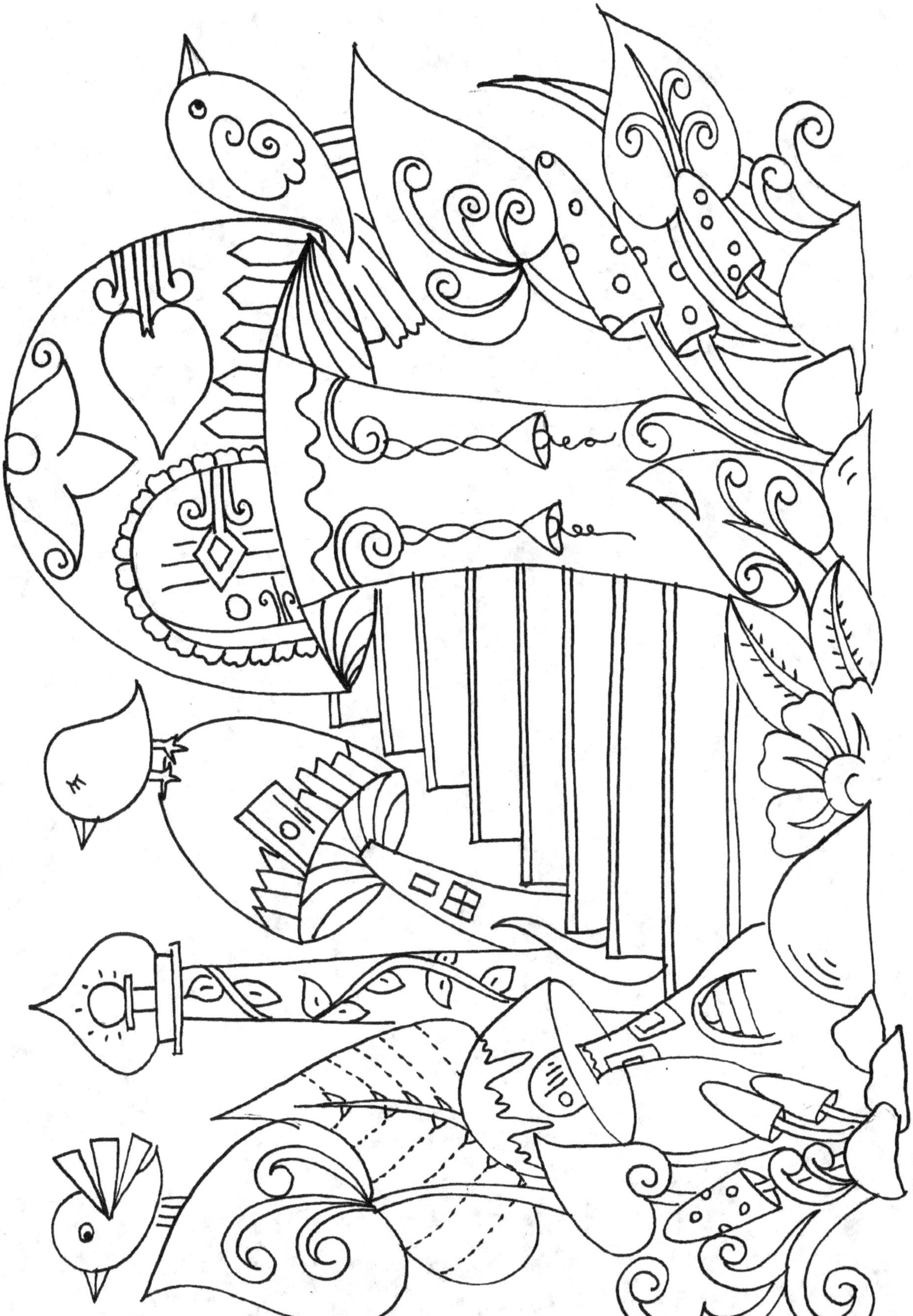

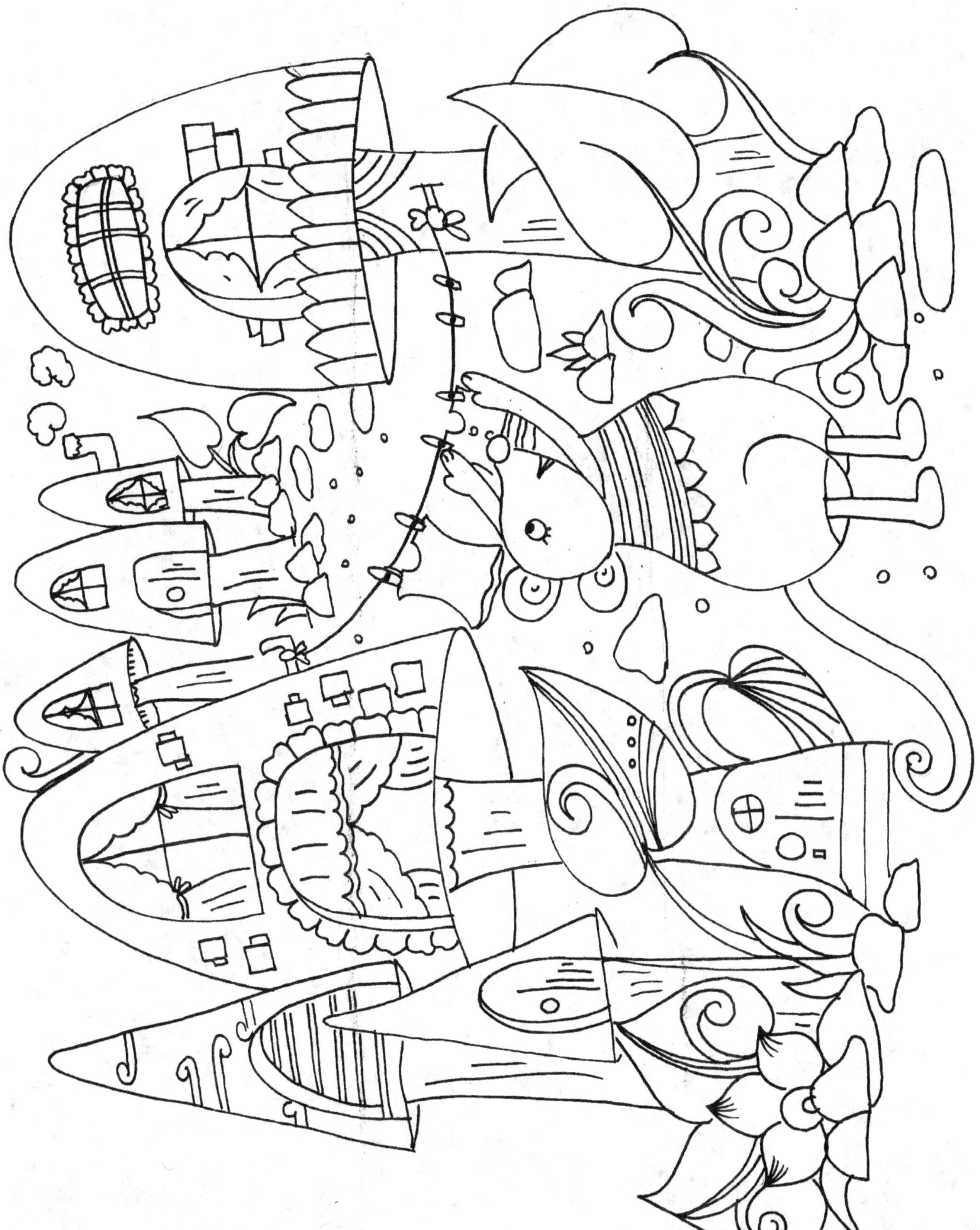

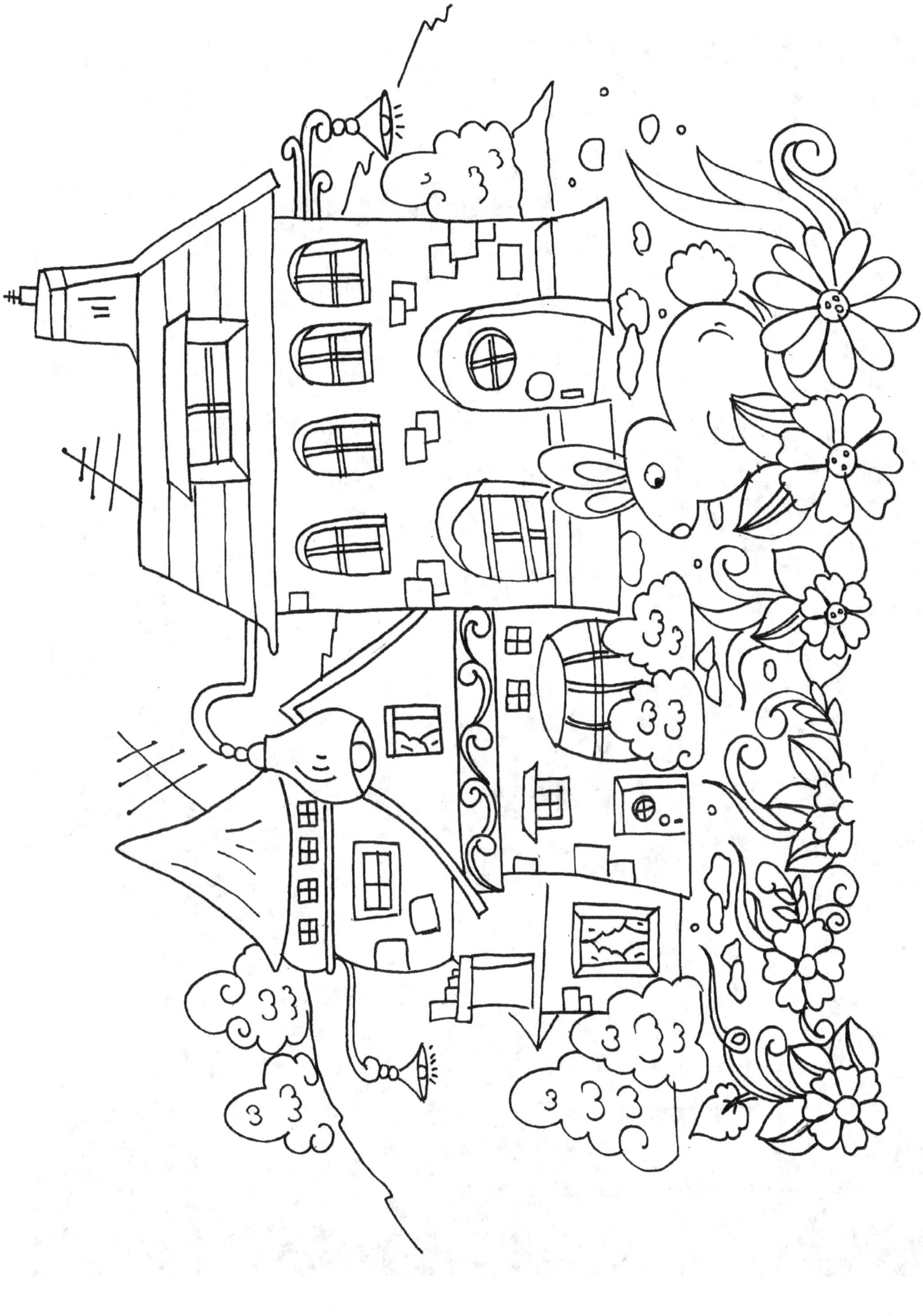

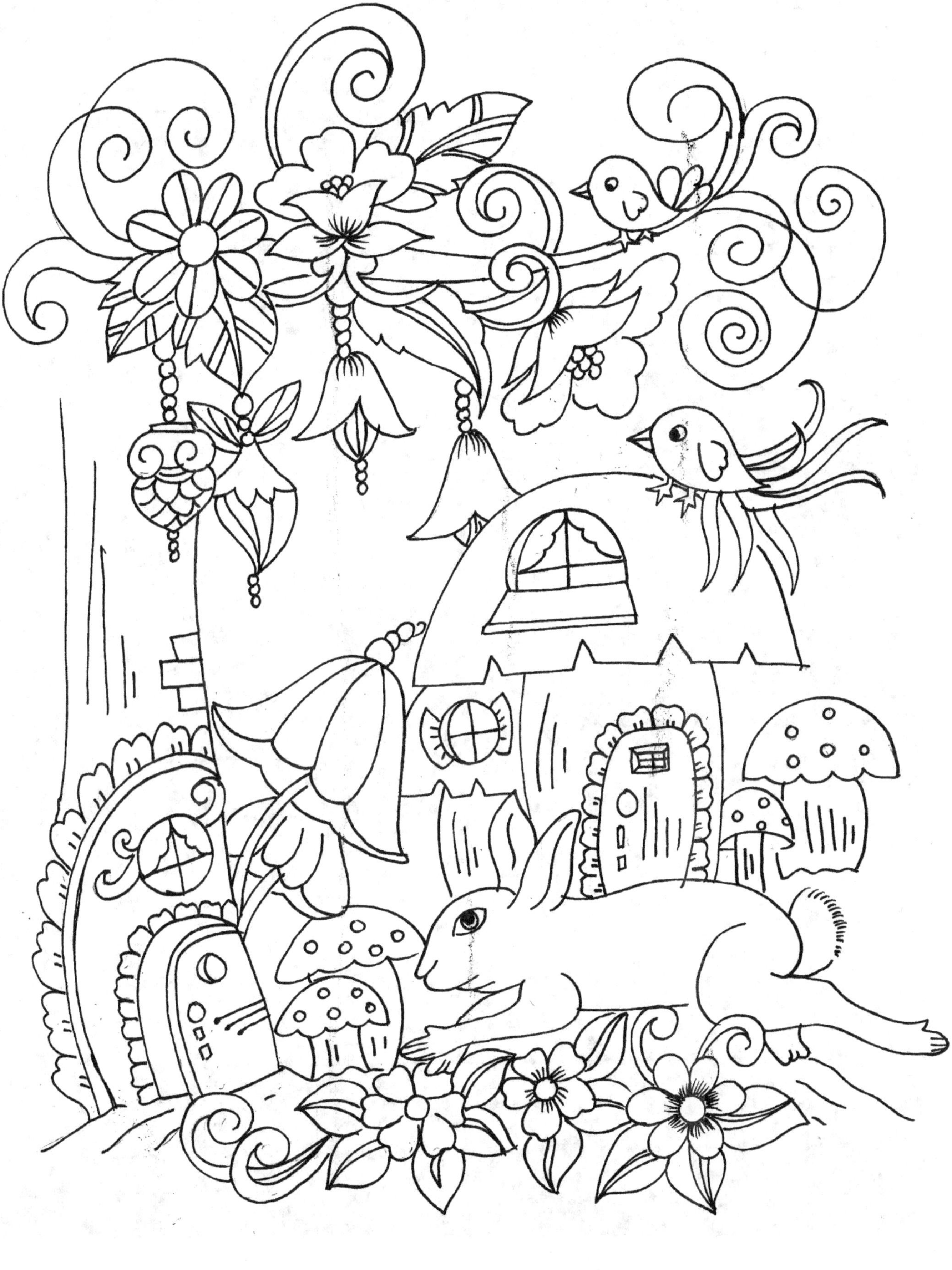

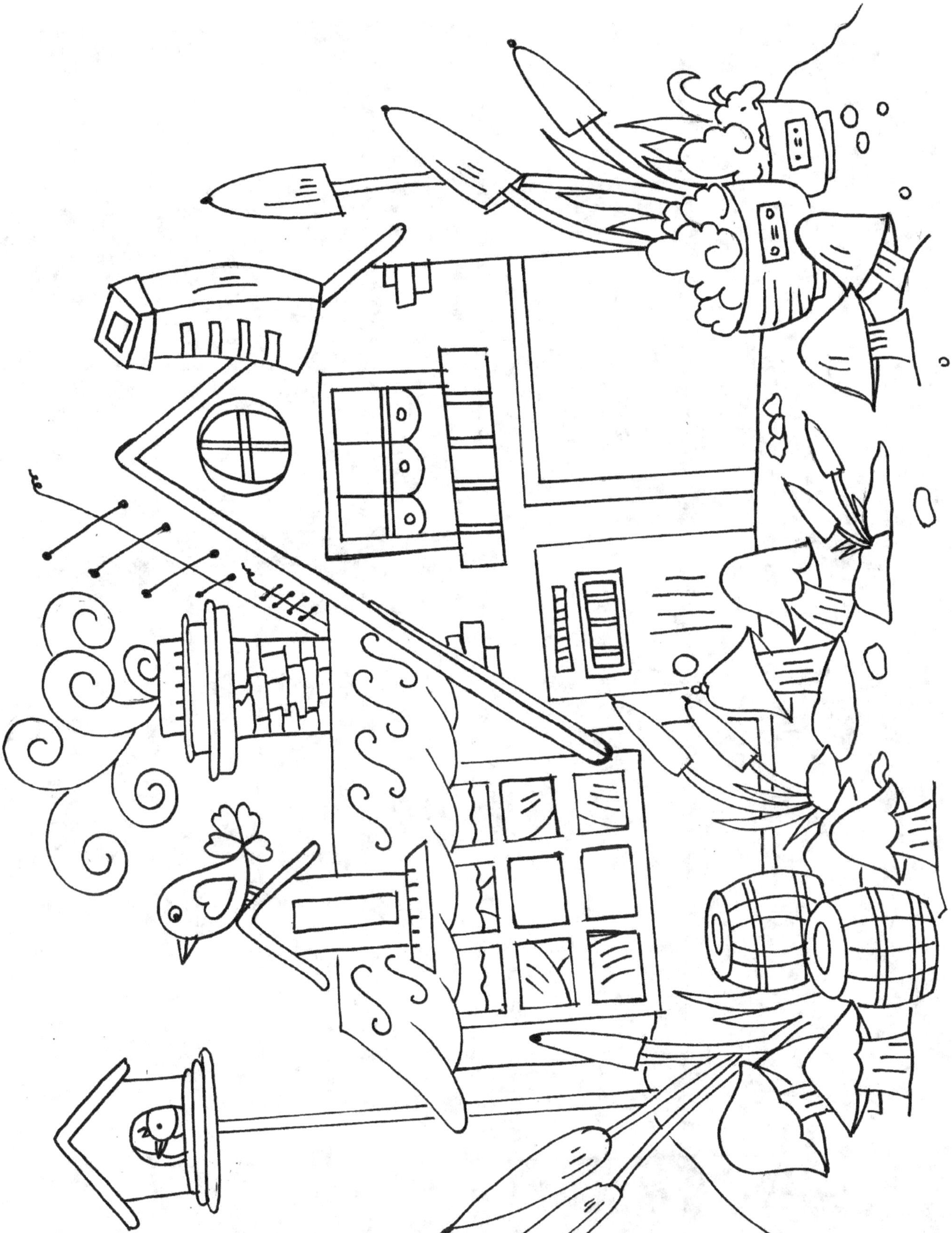

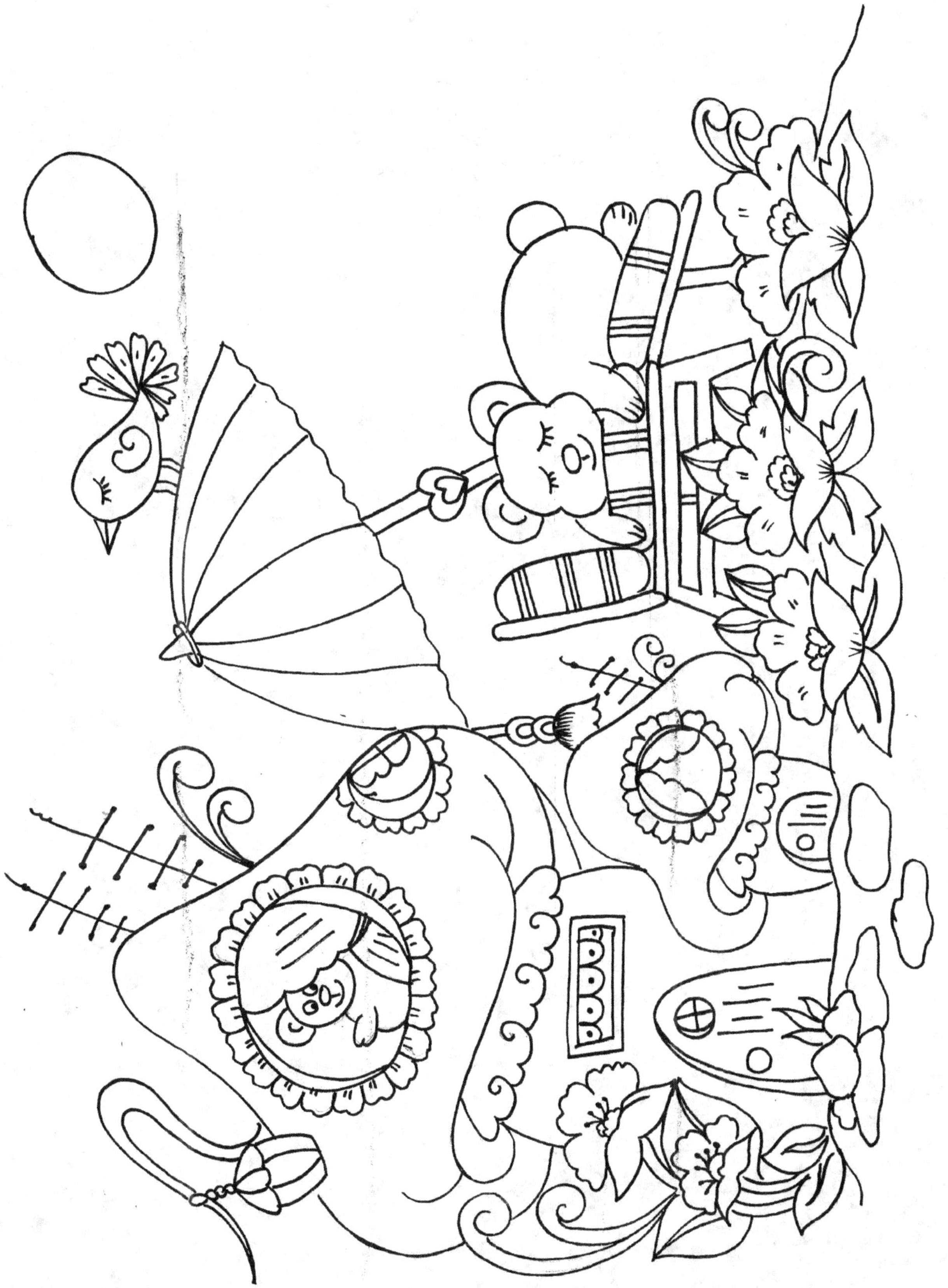

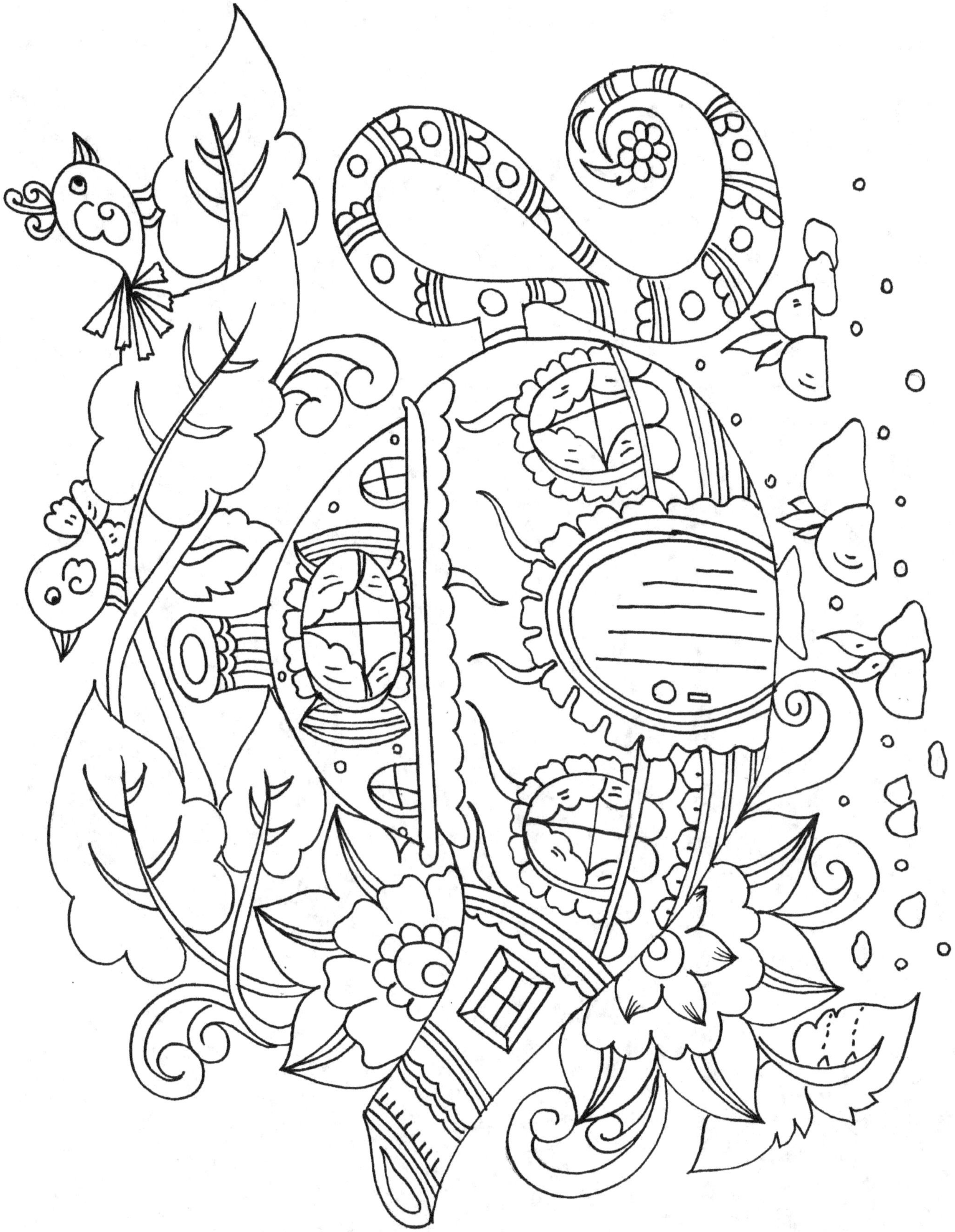

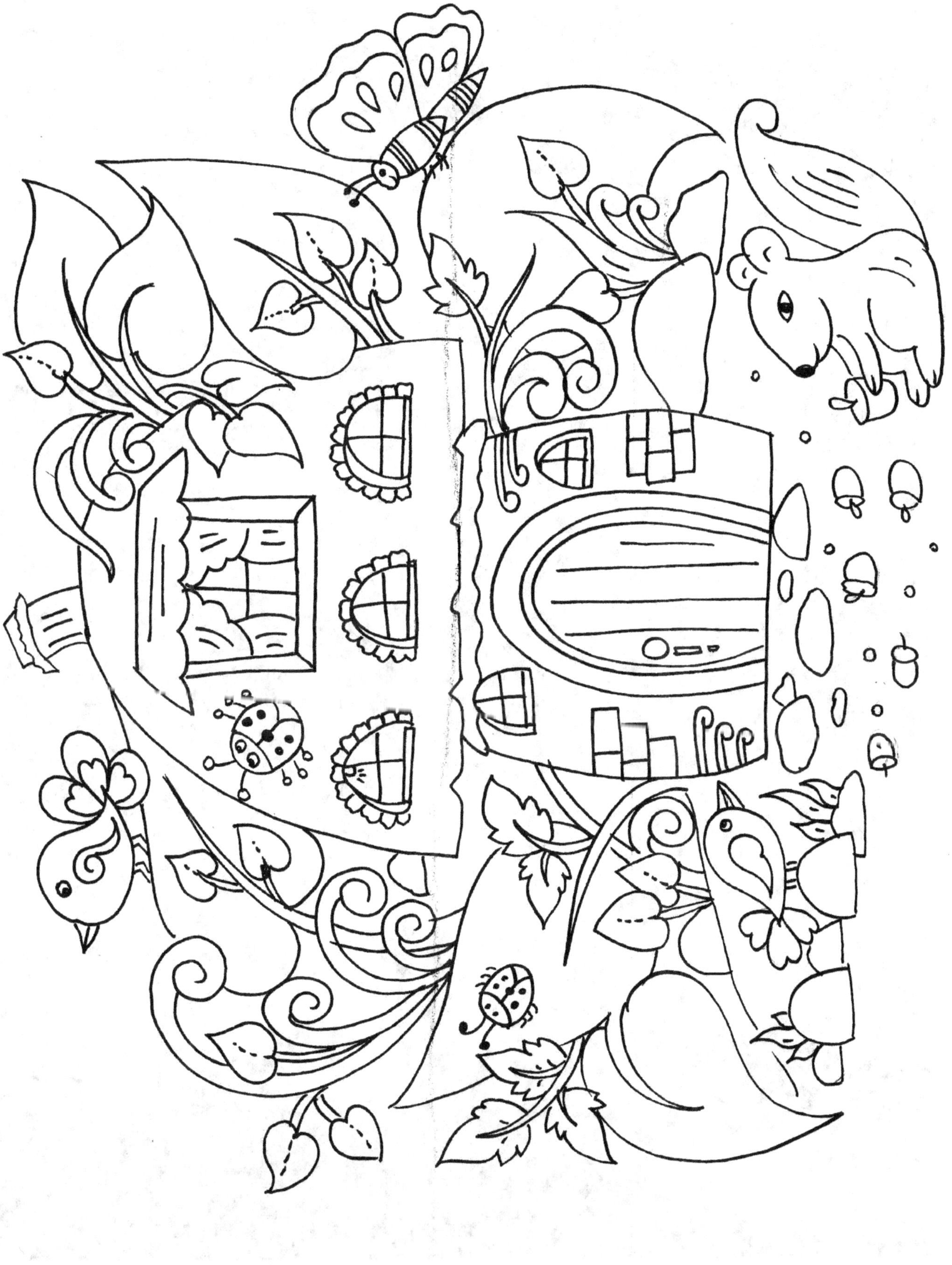

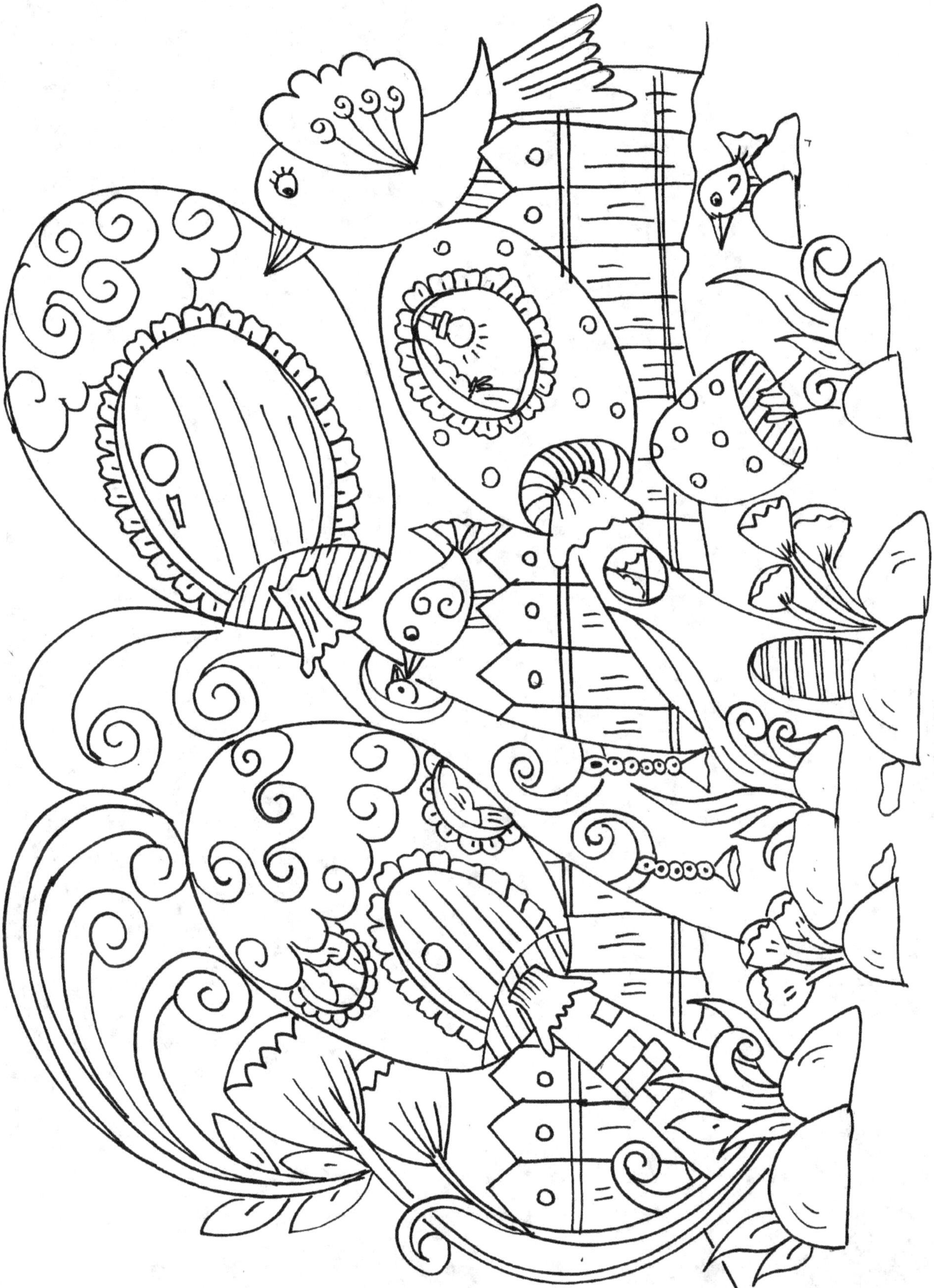

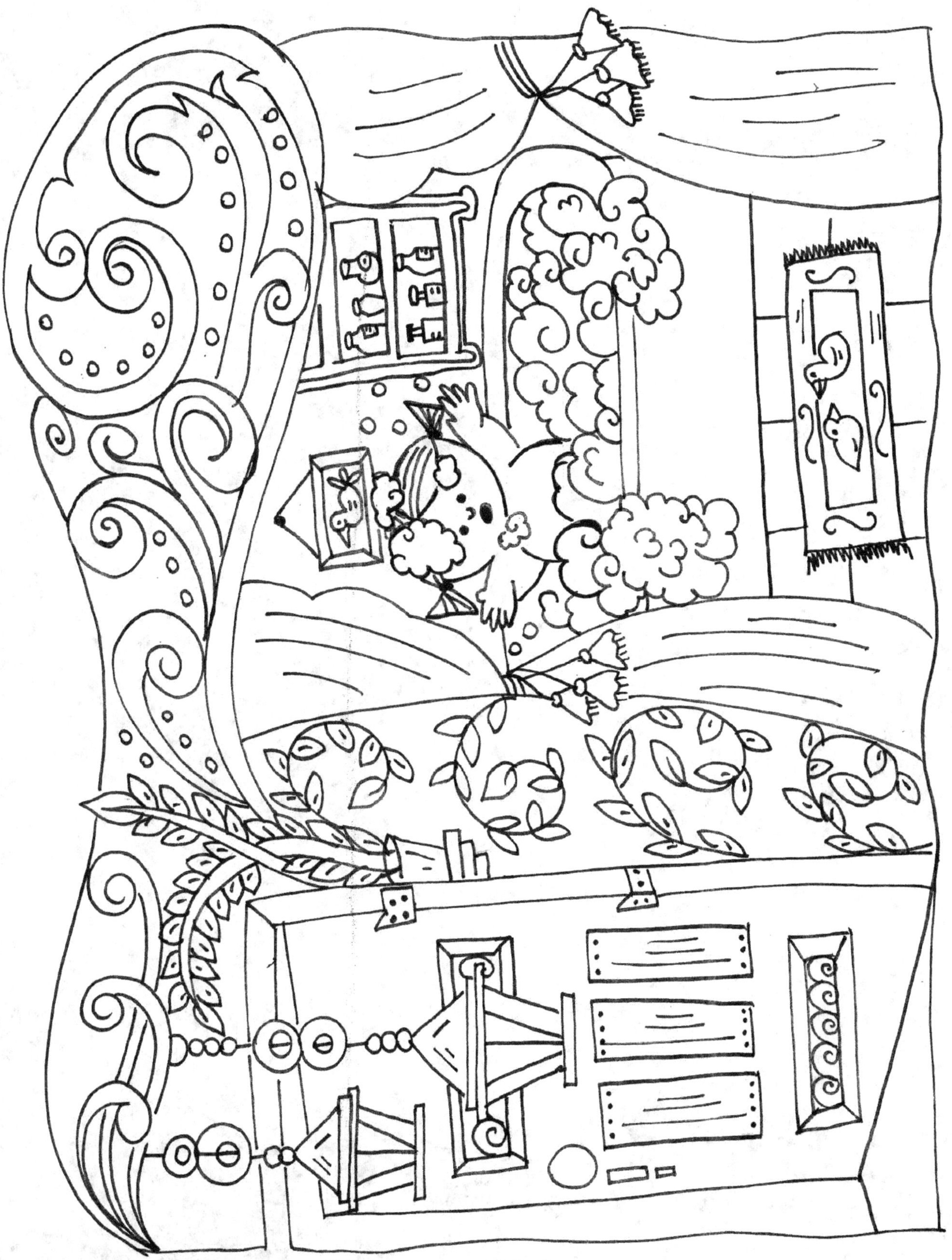

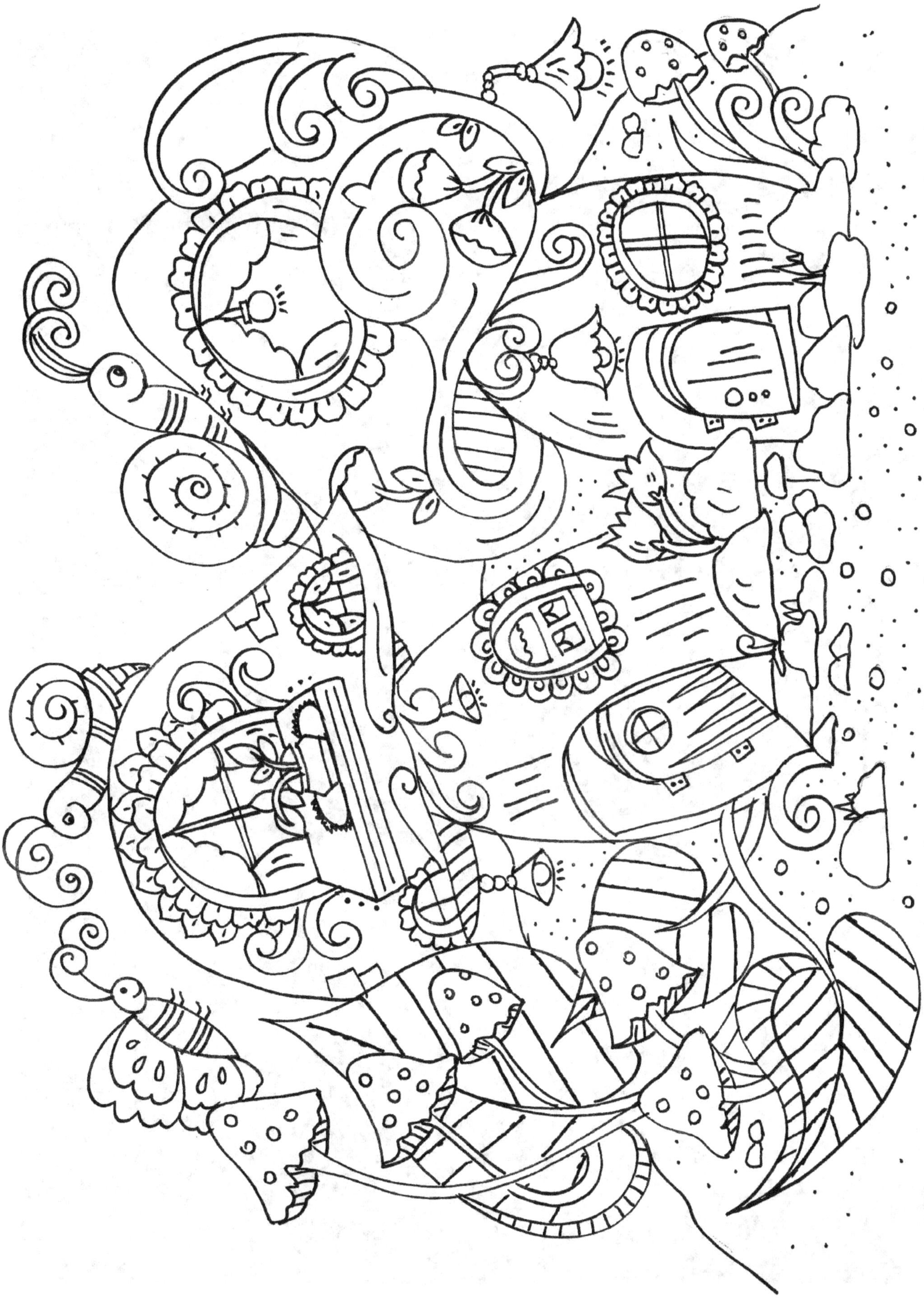

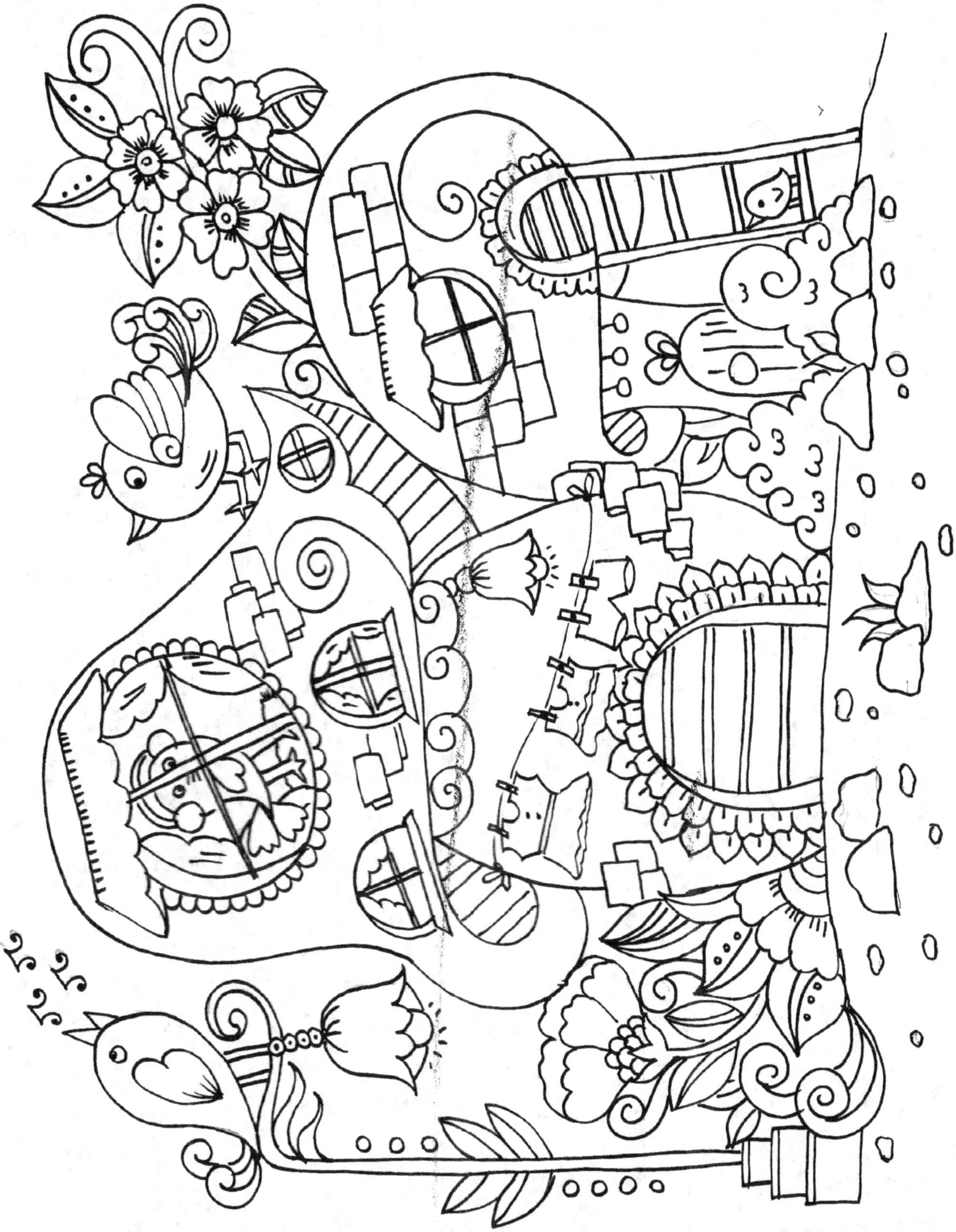

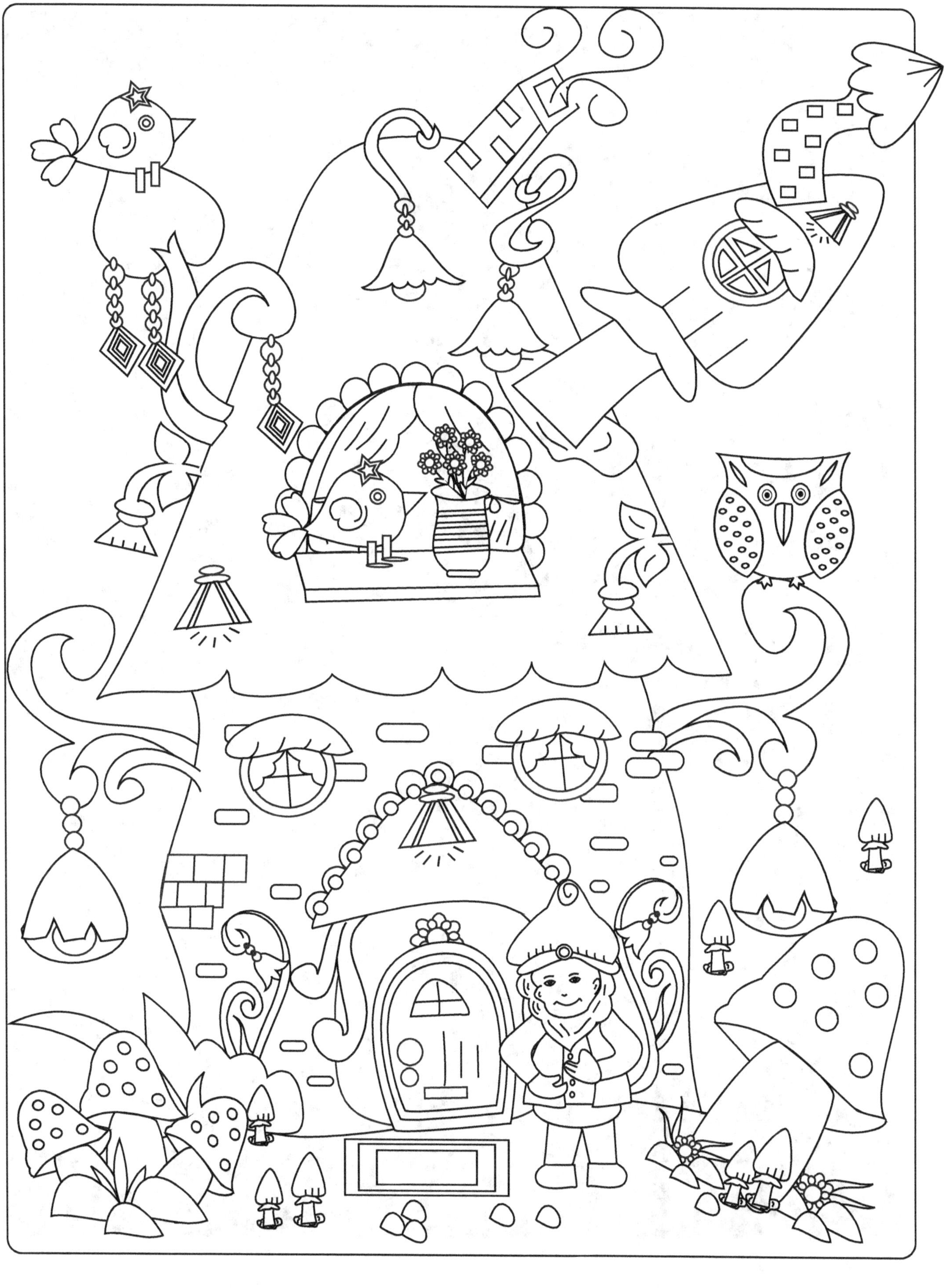

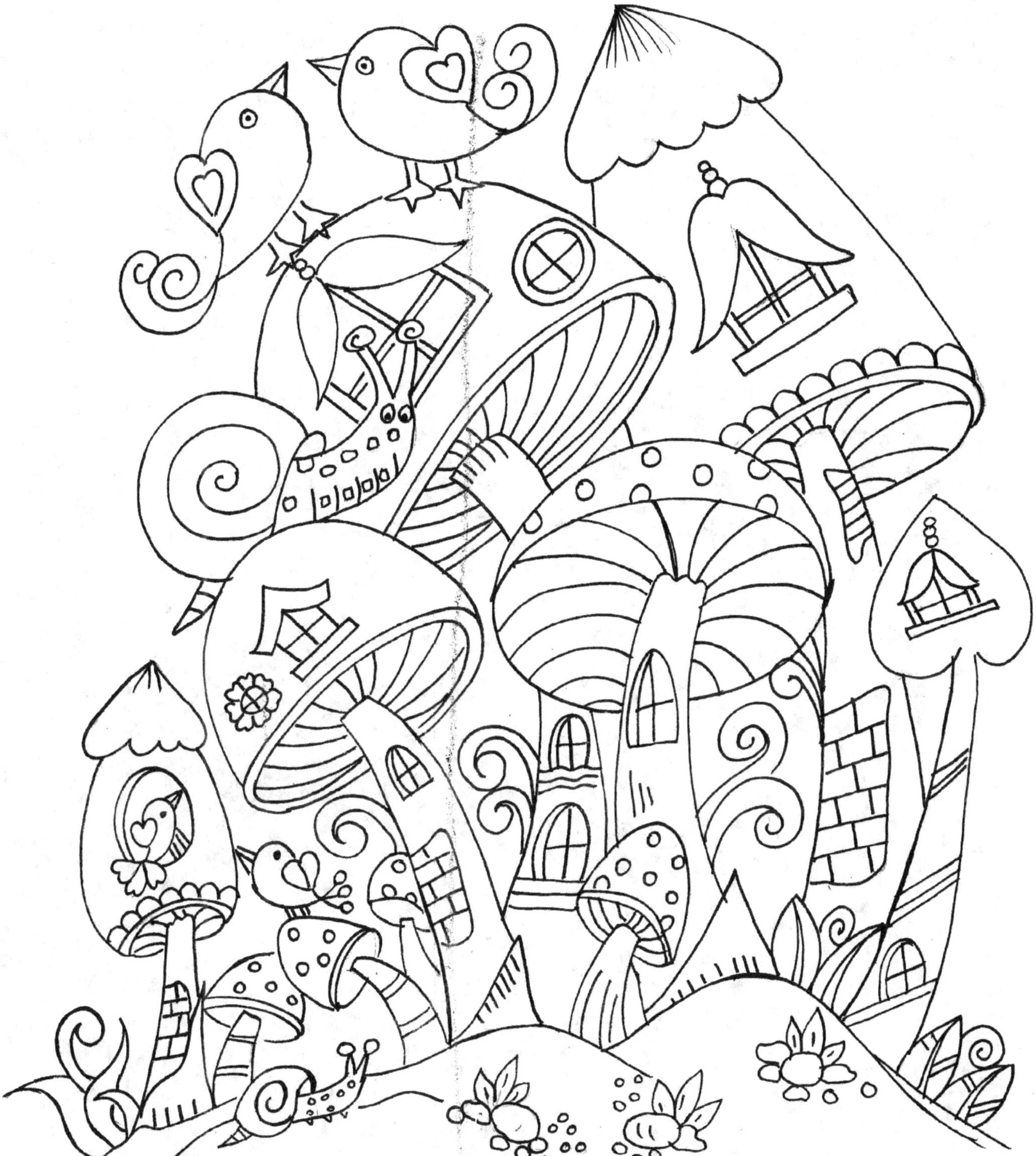

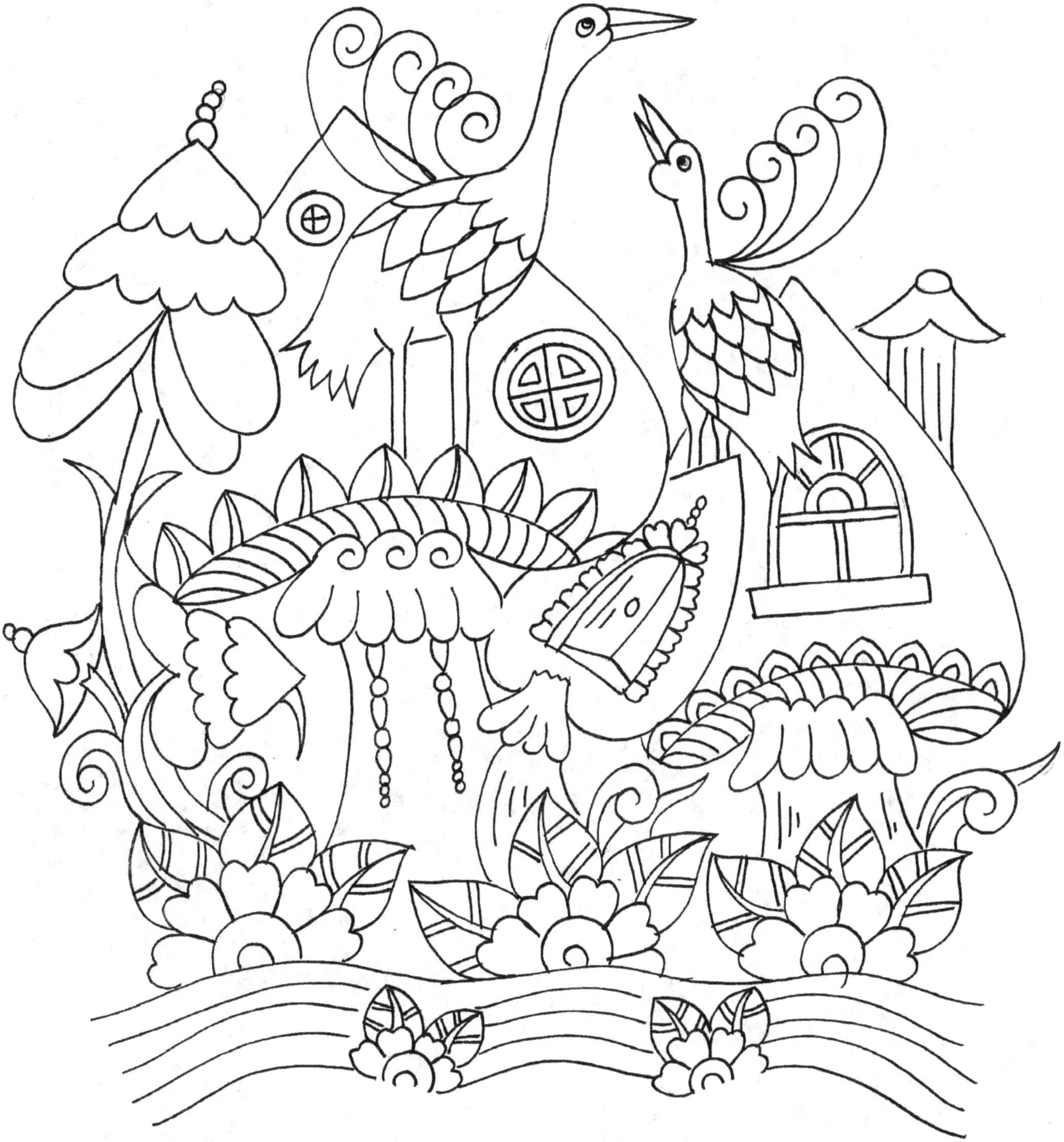

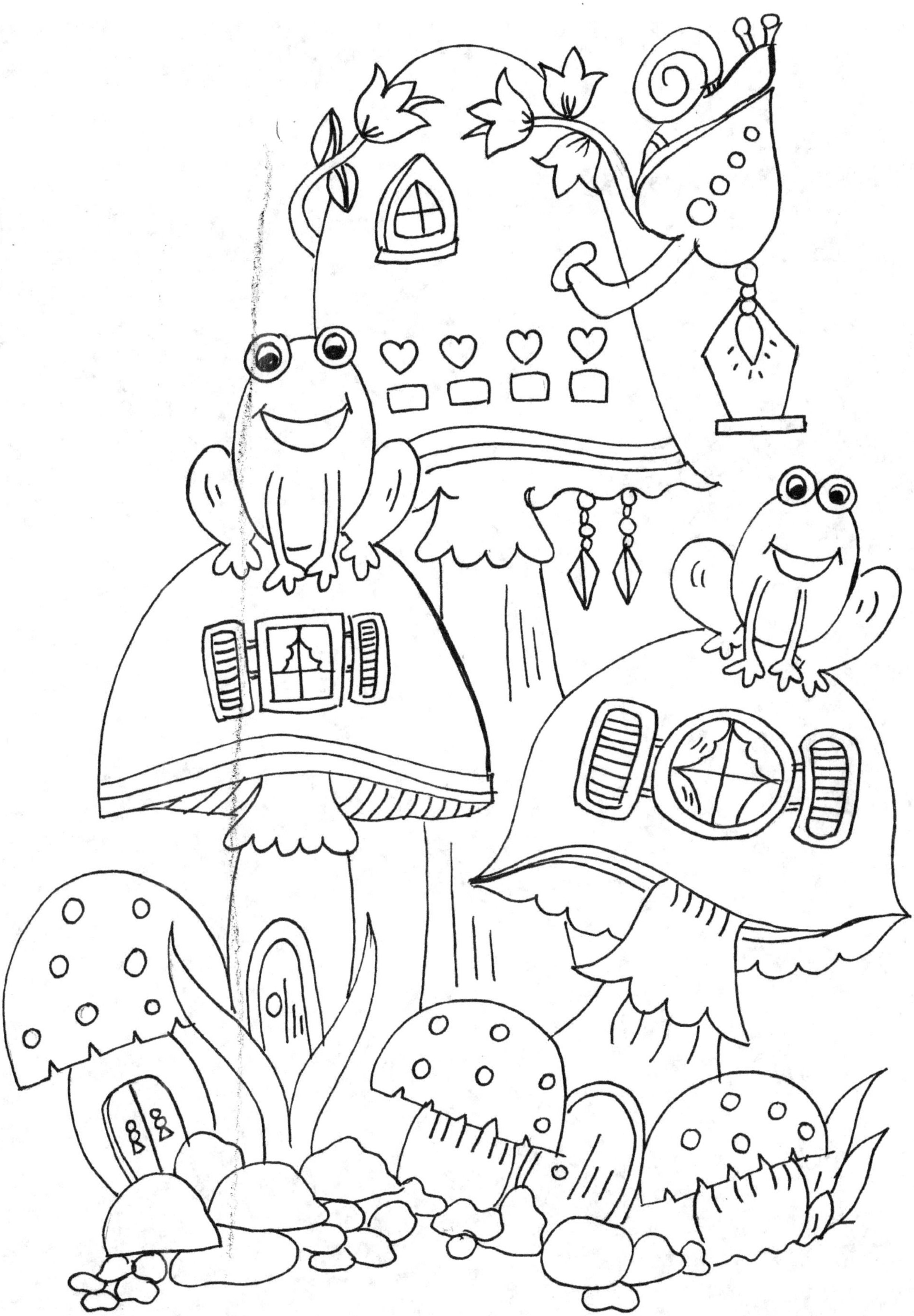

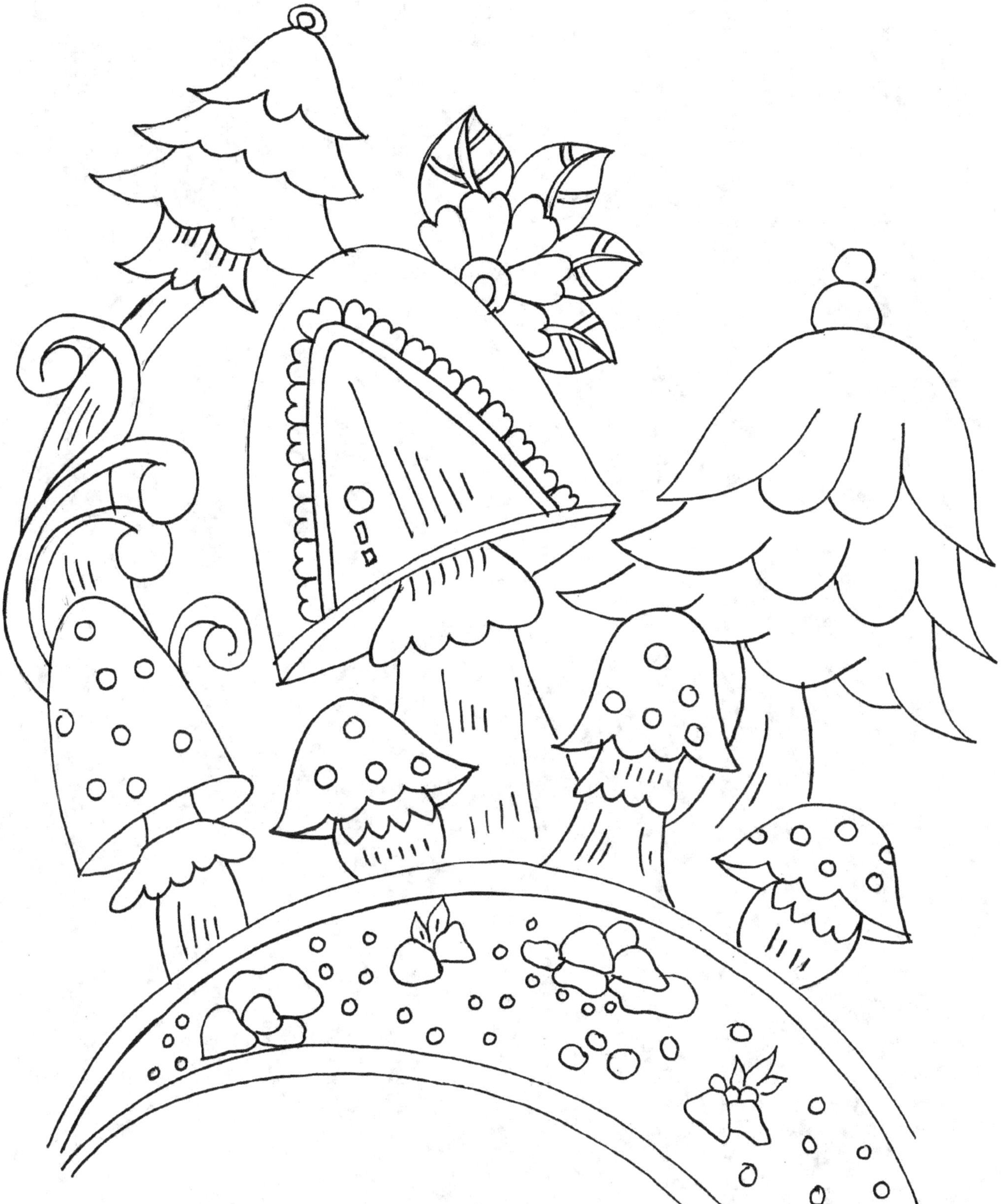

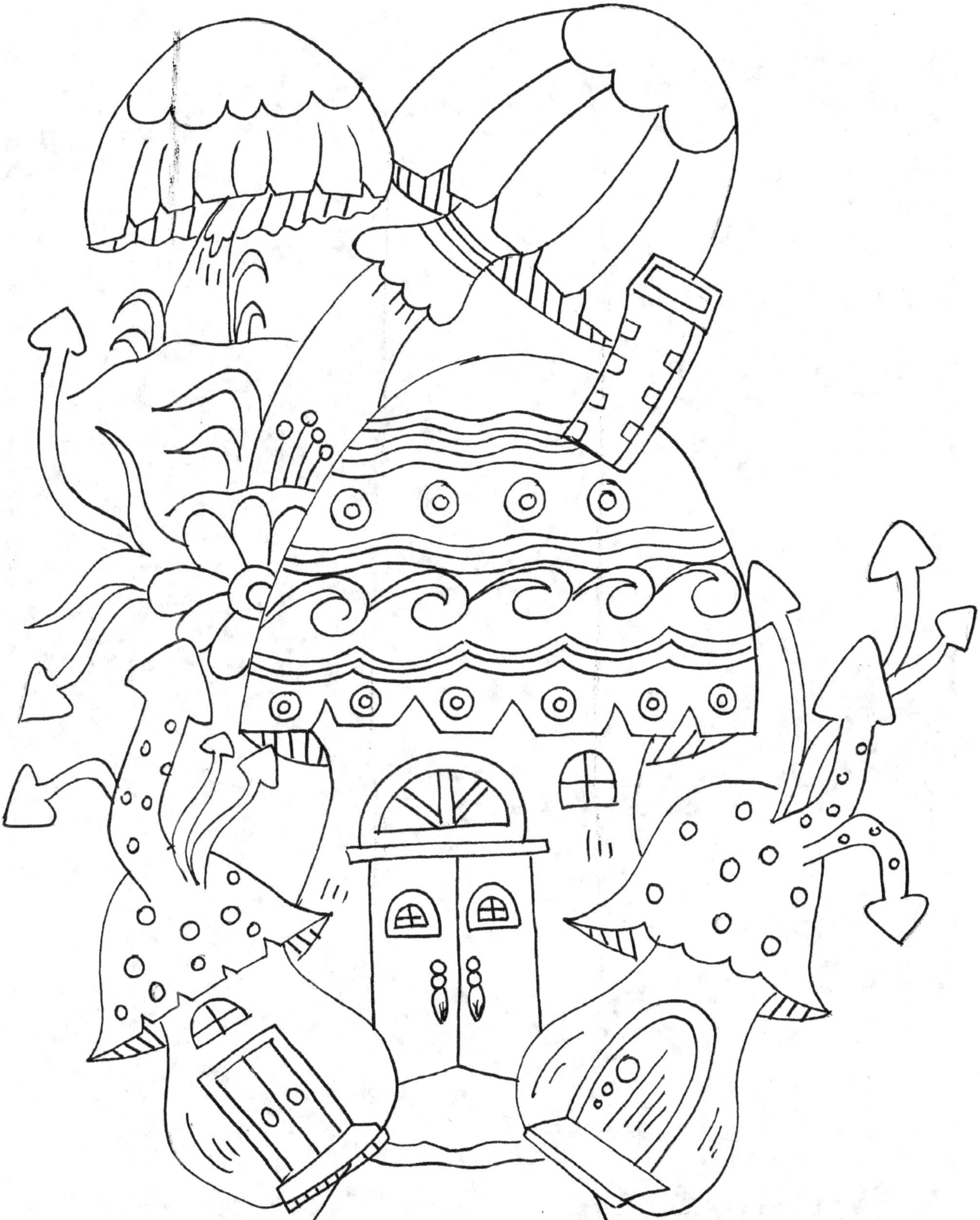

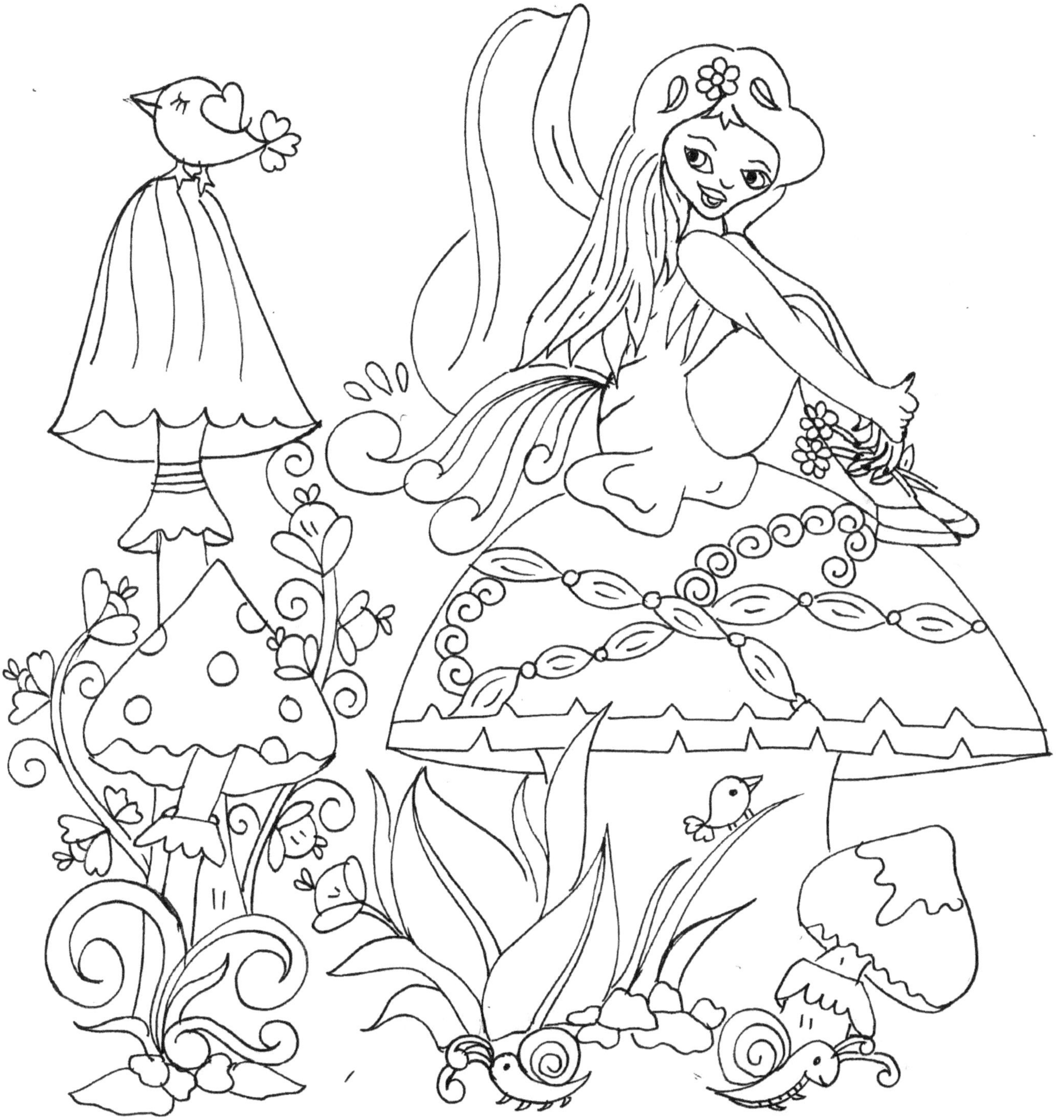

Color test

Color test

www.ingramcontent.com/pod-product-compliance
Lightning Source LLC
Chambersburg PA
CBHW081747220526
45468CB00008B/2275